MY SECRETS FROM HEAVEN

A Child's Trip To Heaven and Back

Susanne Seymoure

ISBN: 0998811912
ISBN 13: 9780998811918

CHAPTER 1

THE KNOT IN THE SCARF

During the winter of January 19, 1975, we were watching out of the window in the Swiss chalet as the day began. Small, light, fluffy snowflakes slowly accumulated all over the ground. I was twelve years old. Little did we know that day would bring events that accumulated just like the snow, and develop into a shocking experience that would change lives forever. For that day I would see Heaven, and when I got older, I would share the secret, a secret I have kept for many years, as my mother didn't feel it was safe to talk about. Now I have been guided to share. It is a duty, a calling, a testimony, and a humble service to make the experience available to benefit anyone interested.

The snowflakes started out soft and small. We were expecting up to two feet of snow that day. Being stuck in the house during the cold winter for too long gave us cabin fever. We were not big TV watchers. We had maybe four channels to choose from, and it didn't take long before we ran out of games to play. My mother Hedy said excitedly, "Hey, why don't we go for a walk and get some exercise and fresh air?" Our family walked together often. One by one, we slowly stood up and stretched, getting ready to "shake a leg." When we got nice and cold, we looked forward to the walk back home to enjoy a nice warm meal together. Walking made us feel like we were doing something good for ourselves.

"Enough of this sitting around," Hedy continued. "We need to get out of this house today, even if it's just for a little while. So let's dress warm, meet downstairs, and walk together in this beautiful snowy forest." Sounded good to us.

After we were all dressed, the women in the family applied face moisturizer for protection as a finishing touch. Then we met downstairs near the front door. Looking around, we noticed the old red skis we bought second hand at a neighbor's yard sale, just sitting in the corner of the cold garage. My brother Robert and I never went skiing before, but we hoped to learn now that the vacation house in the mountains was finished. The community had a free ski hill for members. "Let's bring the skis along on our hike. The kids can take a run down the ski hill. Let's put some use to all this snow." Excitedly and feeling a sense of adventure, I, along with my younger brother Robert, grabbed the old skis and threw them over our shoulders. My father Walter and my grandfather Otto said they would carry them for us. They placed them over their shoulders and smiled. We smiled back with relief. It's great when your parents carry things for you.

Once outside the front door, standing in the driveway and ready to head out for the walk, Hedy turned to me and said, "Wait a minute Susanne. Put a scarf on please. Your neck will get cold."

"I have a scarf on, Mommy; see?" I replied. It was a six-foot-long, brown-and-cream-striped scarf with long cream fringe on each end.

"Well, tie it around your neck. It doesn't do any good to have it just hanging around you."

Makes sense, right? So I tied it around my neck as Hedy said, eager to please her. I loved pleasing my mom. I idolized her. She was my best friend. I trusted everything she ever told me. And of course, I just wanted to get going.

But Hedy wasn't pleased and said, "No, here let me do it." She added another loop swoop and pull to make it a knot. Strangely I got very agitated, as if a bee had just stung me. Something in me was restless.

"What's the matter? Is it too tight?" she asked.

"No, it's not that; I just don't want it tied in a knot."

"That's silly," she replied with a smirk and a shake of her head.

I usually did whatever my mother told me, so the feeling I was having about something that seemed so simple was completely out of character for me. I was usually very pleasing and peaceful, especially when it came to my mother.

"No, I don't want a knot!" I reacted.

We argued, and argued, and argued. After all, what would have been the difference if she had just let me tie it? And why did she want me to tie it into a knot? Ultimately, Hedy wouldn't let us go anywhere unless my scarf was knotted. I stood my ground with many tears, insisting that one pull-through meant it was tied.

"What has gotten into you?" she asked. "This is ridiculous. Why won't you knot that scarf?"

I didn't want it tied at all. Something inside me didn't feel right about the scarf. I kept refusing to tie it. Everyone in the family stared at me with confusion over my reaction.

"Why is she behaving like this over a scarf?"

"What is the matter with her?"

It became a moment that no one in the family ever forgot. It was a moment of instinct. Thanks to this experience, I grew to understand the gift of instinct as some kind of protection around us that we can't see or explain. Have you ever had a moment in your life when you were unwilling to get on a train or an airplane or do something you were supposed to do?

I finally agreed to tie the scarf into a knot, as everyone was getting so impatient and upset. I didn't want to upset everyone else, but I was so upset that my stomach started cramping and I felt as if I was going to vomit. Tearful and confused, I started walking. I couldn't shake that feeling no matter how hard I tried.

"Don't spoil the day," Hedy said.

My brain knew she was right, but my gut was still nauseated and shaky.

Very strange, I thought.

We began walking up the driveway. I was hoping the beauty of the snowfall would help me shake off the nausea, but it didn't happen. I was determined to have a good time as best I could, but I felt upset all the way to the hill. I shook my head, still confused about why I could not control this reaction. It was so eerie it gave me chills.

We walked in the snow; appreciating its beauty; and deeply breathing in the cold, fresh, clean air. Each individual tree branch was covered in snow. Mother nature is such an artist. We all loved nature and soaked up all she had to offer with so much appreciation for the details, as we walked about five miles to get to the hill we were going to use for our skiing.

The snow was now changing from millions of small, blistery flakes, to large chunks that began to cover the ground quickly. We had brought our dog, Heidi. The snow accumulated to about a foot, and we noticed the miniature schnauzer becoming increasingly tired as she struggled to hop over it. The snow got so deep that the road and the forest blended together. No snowplows were around that day. So we decided to take a "shortcut" through the woods. Heidi did her best to leap over the blueberry shrubs and vastly accumulating snowfall. A small but spirited dog, she kept up as long as she could. Every now and then Walter would pick her up and carry her for a much-needed rest. Then he would put her down again and she'd once again resume hopping alongside us, until she got tired again and started lagging behind. We were growing tired, as well, so we became increasingly comfortable believing, *She is coming,* or *She is back there somewhere,* and turned around less and less to try to see her. Eventually we got to the point we could barely walk, as our legs began to weaken and the buildup of lactic acid plus the cold air kept us challenged. Our breathing became heavier. We could see each other breathe clouds in the frigid air, and it became more difficult to talk as we walked. Robert and I were walking in our stiff ski boots.

At one point I thought, *Now I understand how people can just lay down, fall asleep, and freeze to death in the snow.* We were completely exhausted, but home was now too far away. All of a sudden there came Otto's words, right out of Hedy's mouth: "There is no such thing as 'I can't.'" Toughness and an athletic spirit were in our blood. We marched on, feeling we were giving our bodies a good workout instead of a dormant slumber back at the house. We got lost for quite a while, though, then once again became very frustrated. By this time, we were feeling sympathetic toward one another, as defeat was slowly sinking in, followed by a touch of helplessness. All the trees, markings, and roads were so heavily covered in the snow, and the snowflakes constantly landing on our eyelashes made it difficult to see. *Eyelashes, the windshield wiper of the eyes,* I began thinking, *couldn't keep up even with us blinking rapidly.* What a blizzard! No one was outside: not a car, a person, or a deer. The silence was overwhelming. The only sound was the wind blowing, sometimes gently, sometimes strongly. The cold biting air on our faces made it difficult for us to even open our mouths. We were frozen, our clothes stiff and wet, and our feet and hands numb. Scared in a way that made us more respectful of the weather, we knew we had to get to the hill quickly, hoping the clubhouse would be open.

We saw the hill from a distance, ramped up one more time, and used our last burst of energy to get there. My thighs were burning hot inside, even though I was in good shape, being a swimmer and a gymnast. Actually, all of us hiked frequently. My grandparents would hike in the Alps in their younger days. Nevertheless, we were exhausted like we had never been before. We got to the point where we were almost crawling to the hill.

CHAPTER 2

THE ENTANGLED SCARF

Finally, we had made it to the bottom of the approximately 2,000-foot-long slope covered in a white snow blanket. The snow was untouched.

It was a private community, not open to the public. We saw the large brown clubhouse to the right side of the hill. It offered a moment of warmth and rest, but Walter checked and it was locked up. *Sigh,* he breathed, and went on to say "But there is a guy up there with the keys, a big ring of keys."

"Hey," Hedy said, "maybe he can turn on the ski lift for us." Walter knew Hedy wouldn't back down from an idea, so he didn't waste time trying to persuade her from it. "Quick," she said, "I'll go with you and we can ask him."

They tried their best to not let us be disappointed that we couldn't ski. Truth is, by that point, we really didn't care. But as parents they knew better. They knew that once we children would actually see the towrope ski lift working, even if we were exhausted, we would get a second wind. That's the beauty of a child's energy; there is always time to sleep later.

"Success!" Hedy shouted from the top of the hill down to us. "He said he will open it for us, and turn it on!" He used the key and demonstrated how to use the on and off switch inside the booth. He went on to say "Just return the key to me when you are finished." The key was the only way to turn it off and allowed us to ski as long as we wanted. The man was so cold he thought we were nuts to be out in this weather. He scurried home to his warm house on foot, leaving a path of new footprints in the untouched snow on the roads. No cars were on the road, and he didn't live that far away. But even though he looked at us as if we were absolutely crazy, my parents told him we paid dues to use it. Couldn't argue with skiers on a snowy day.

Defeat turned to success. We felt so lucky that we had run into the only other person we saw that day beside ourselves. A new excitement and outlook emerged as though we had never walked all that way. We forgot how tired we were. The ski lift had a towrope made of medium blue nylon, the frays of which could poke through our gloves. It was a towrope ski lift, or sometimes called a pulley ski lift, and the blue rope ran along the ground. We had never used one before, but curiously it looked simple and helpful to pull our tired, wet, noodle legs up the hill we now didn't have to climb. Now that we could use the rope lift, we could get up the hill faster and spend more time skiing.

The rope was a stranger to us all. Curiously Robert picked it up off the ground first. It jerked him so fast he looked like it gave him whip lash. He laughed nervously and said, "This thing is crazy, but I think we can do it." We were scared by the power the lift had. He fell a few times, but kept trying. The rope had such a strong force that we had to be ready to be pulled fast and hard. Metal poles, the height of telephone poles, supported the pulley rope. At the top of the hill was a booth that resembled a large garden shed or some kind of shack. Inside the booth was a machine that had large interlocking wheeled gears that pulled the rope from the ground and then threw it out on top to come down the high metal poles. It was a simple pulley mechanism, though the gears looked as if they were eight feet tall. Robert and I walked up the hill at first to check out the shack. "Let's check out this booth and see how the rope goes in," Robert said. Curiosity caused us to look through the small square opening at the bottom to see where the rope went in. Robert said, "Do you think our heads could fit in the opening?" It was very small. 'You might fit your head in there, but I'm not so sure. It is scary though," Robert said. Bending down to look we saw the large metal wheels that turned and pulled the rope. The rope came out way up high, as the poles stood as high as telephone poles. When we grabbed the rope at the bottom of the hill, we had to try not to hit the poles to the left side of us. .

Robert and I eventually got the hang of the rope lift, even though it was much too strong and overpowering for our tired little bodies. Even though we never got comfortable with it, we talked ourselves into fighting the fear of it. I skied down the hill first, and then Robert followed. We fell a few times, but got up and laughed, trying to become one with these "long feet" called skis. What fun it was. We all got a burst of energy and almost forgot the snow was still rapidly falling. Robert said, 'Let's keep trying again and again." With a smile of surprise I replied, "Okay." Our tracks were the only ones on that snow-covered hill, and they were covered almost as soon as we finished coming down. Below was a flat area where Otto, Maya, Walter, and Hedy waited to cheer as we came down, as they were too exhausted to walk up the hill. Each time we came down the hill they cheered. So they unselfishly stood and froze in the frigid air as they shared the joy in providing this moment for their children. It was their way of offering a better childhood than they had had.

After going down the three-tiered hill, laughing and shouting, "Watch me"; "Watch this"; we were getting into a groove of skiing better and better. We almost felt as if we weren't beginners anymore since we felt we knew how to do it. When we were on top of the hill you could not see the second tier or third and bottom tier.

We skied down the first tier then it leveled off, then a second hill and then it also leveled off before reaching a third hill. At the bottom of the third hill is where the parents and grandparents waited.

Smiling and racing to go up the hill together, I went first and Robert agreed to wait a minute before grabbing the rope. That way, if I fell he would not crash into me. I picked up the rope at the bottom of the hill after seeing my parents and grandparents smile at me. I took the jolt, but stayed standing on my skis with good balance. After a minute, I was confident enough to look back over my right shoulder for my brother and tell him it was his turn to grab the rope.

"Good job," I said after he grabbed it.

"I'm coming, Sue," he replied.

I turned to face forward with a steady stance, such pride and relief in my new ability. I was excited and happy looking up the hill, anticipating the next downhill run.

Unexpectedly, I felt my head jerk forward with a force that at first left me standing and then made me look at where I had placed my hand on the rope. The fringe on my scarf had also decided to hold onto the rope. As the rope spun in a spiral forward motion, in a similar direction to wringing out a towel, I noticed my scarf was also being spun around the rope. I had no time for this silliness and I tried to untangle it, but the rope was faster than my hands. For a moment I was confident I could get the fringe unhooked, but the speed made it impossible and my adrenaline kicked in. I went from merely being annoyed to fight or flight mode within a few seconds.

"Uh oh" I said to myself as I realized there was no one in the booth to shut the mechanism off. As the rope pulled the scarf very quickly in a forward and spiral fashion, I remembered Robert behind me, and I felt safe for a second. In an effort to spare him from what I thought would be horrifying for him to see, I yelled back and screamed, "let go of the rope."

"Let go of the rope!" I said again, seeing that I was in life-threatening trouble. Robert replied, "I'm coming! Don't worry, Sue; I'm coming!"

I tried to pull the scarf over my head but it was too tight. I tried to loosen the knot in the scarf—the knot I didn't want to tie in the first place! The argument with my mom flashed in my mind. I knew now that the instincts I had earlier were probably for this reason. If it had just been the one loop through and pull, I could have loosened it, but no, it was a double knot that Hedy insisted I wear. Too late now to focus on that so I decided to try with the fight of a tiger to loosen it, but knew it was impossible. I didn't give up or panic, though. I fought for my life trying to be smart, strong, and focused. But quickly time ran out as well as oxygen, and had to put my hand between my neck and the scarf to block the increasing asphyxiation. It took a lot of strength to hold my hand against the tightening scarf. I felt as if the bones in my hand were breaking and my neck was being crushed. . I fell to the ground and it was now an official hanging, a good old-fashioned rope hanging. It flipped me around by my neck and my head was hitting every pole on the way up. I tried to grab the rope again, gasping for air. Seeing each pole come near, I tried to keep my head and body from making contact. But each time I saw another pole coming, I hit them all head on, despite all my efforts to flail my head and body to avoid them. In between the hits, the square cutout in the booth entered my mind. *Will my head fit through it?* I wondered, *Or am I going to be decapitated when my head gets stuck? Maybe my head will go through it only to be crushed in the gears.* There didn't seem to be a happy ending, and I hoped more than anything that my brother wouldn't see this. I didn't know at the time he had fallen off less than halfway up and could no longer see me.

I knew there was no logical way I could stop this. And I now knew that my life would end when my head hit the booth square. I saw it coming faster and faster. A strange courage in facing my death approached. I felt an acceptance in facing mortality. I wanted to be sure I had given it my absolute best shot in the world. *I'm not going without a fight,* I remember thinking, and when I lost the fight I decided I would have no regret because I knew I had done all I could, right up to the moment of death. Win or lose, live or die, I had done my best.

"Get ready; here it comes," I said to myself as I mentally prepared for the end. I still had a ways to go and began to count down the seconds.... "This is it,".... Silence.

I died shortly before making contact with the towrope booth. I hit the booth but I don't remember the impact. I know I hit it because when I awoke, my head was against the bottom of the towrope booth. But I felt no pain. I didn't feel anything but silence.

After I opened my eyes, I saw softly falling snowflakes in a gray sky with air blowing the newly fallen snow around in swirls lifting it from the ground. I felt alone for a short moment before I heard what sounded like someone coming toward me. The experience I was about to have would change my life forever, and it may change yours, too. I saw my short twelve-year-old life flash before me. It was a life review that showed me highlights that my heart carried. It pulled the loving feelings in my heart into images. I swiftly began to recognize how much we are all a part of each other, how we are all entangled in each other's lives. I received an overwhelming feeling of how we are all connected. All living things are connected. What happens to one impacts all loved ones, like the rings in a lake when a pebble is thrown.

My grandparents, my parents, and my brother, completely believed I died a horrific death on that hill, as the logic of that accident led to no other choice. Maya, my grandmother begged my mother Hedy not to go to me yet. She said, "No mother should see their child that way." They all decided it would be too gruesome to see my dead mangled body, and waited for Walter to run to the nearest house. They hoped he would get help or get to a phone for help. Little did they know, I was not alone, but in the best of hands.

This is the story of a family, their beliefs formed by their own early life experiences, meaningfully entangled, with love as the driving healing force. Every family has their good and bad. See the love and light that is given. Then, take the dark negativity like trash and put it on the curb. We are all a work in progress. Families are also often our first relationships, our first loves, and a place we hope to learn to practice love, faith, communication, understanding, forgiveness, and acceptance. Creating a loving family is a great achievement. Each life brings value.

CHAPTER 3

HEDY'S CHILDHOOD

Hedy, my mother, was an amazing survivor—of war. In fact, her full name, Hedwig, means "war." Interesting how we choose names, carry names, and research the history and meanings of names. How curious when we sometimes really fit our names. She was a tall, slender woman with light brown hair, grey-green eyes, and a large-mouthed smile full of straight, white teeth. Her mane of hair was like that of a lioness. She even had feline manners. When she embraced you she made you feel like you were the only person in the room. Her laughter was strong, loud, contagious, and frequent. She was an expressive person, showing herself and sharing her opinions openly.

Born in 1933 and living her childhood in wartime Germany, she saved all her stories until she felt I was old enough to understand their lessons. "There is no pride in war" Hedy would say, "no real winners; everyone loses." She told me stories of her mother, Maya, and her father, Karl, who were young lovers from the German countryside. They married as teens, practically children, and then Hedy was born.

Maya was from a large family and Karl was an orphan. They loved each other, but on too many occasions, Hedy saw them fight viciously and violently to the point of Karl once holding Maya by the ankles and hanging her out the window. They were frustrated and young and Karl being an orphan had no real examples of love while growing up. "Just awful for a child to see," Hedy said with residual fright in her voice. Karl wasn't always angry, though. He was always kind to Hedy, and he was even funny, often sitting her on his knee and telling her stories to make her laugh.

When he had his sorrowful memories of his time in the orphanage, he would frequent the local beer pub in the evenings. Hedy discovered a way to sneak out of her house to look for him, and one evening saw him through the window at the local pub.

Maya was busy working as a seamstress. Sometimes from their crowded and small apartment located in the low-income area, and Hedy remembers seeing the prostitutes hanging their nylons, chewing gum, wearing red lipstick and high heels, and standing provocatively in front of the cluster of buildings they shared. Hedy had a key around her neck and walked home from school. Maya had her fabrics and clothing spread out on the kitchen table and was sewing to make ends meet. She worked late one night, so Hedy sneaked out again and went to the pub to sit on her father's jovial lap for a few moments before he asked her to go home. It was one of the last times she saw him. He died shortly thereafter at a very young age, some type of lung condition they said, probably pneumonia.

The morning he was buried was rainy and gray. The weather was damp and cool, and everyone at the funeral was wearing raincoats. Hedy remembers standing by the grave under an umbrella that Maya shared with her while her father was lowered into the ground. While under the dripping umbrella, Maya bent down and whispered in Hedy's ear, "Don't cry; be a brave girl." If Maya could have only realized how Hedy needed to cry and ached to be embraced. Hedy stayed hopeful and waited for that embrace, but it did not happen. Despite this, Hedy was very close to her mother.

After Hedy lost her father Karl, she became a clingy, insecure child. It was terrible for Hedy to loose her father, she hated being separated from him and now it was permanent. Maya remained distant because she was busy working and putting food on the table. Maya could have returned home to her very large family in the country but she had left home to live in the city and had her pride, so she continued to try and make it work. Within a short but respectable time, a new man came to visit. His name was Otto, and he was a tall, handsome, quiet, and nostalgic young man. He was an engineer who came from a prominent family. It was said his family owned a large department store chain. He spent time with Maya and Hedy, and he and Maya fell deeply in love. Otto stood over six feet tall and was very distinguished. Maya was five feet tall. Hedy said they would sit on the couch in their small one-room apartment, and he would smoke a cigar as she watched and studied him closely, growing jealous of him sitting so close to her mom. She wanted to be close to Maya and once again Hedy felt separated from a parent. She felt the two of them had eyes only for each other. Hedy remembers when she tried to sit in the middle of her mother and Otto on the couch, Otto teasingly said, "She is all mine now." Hedy feared losing her mom, so Otto's comment only made her fears grow. She panicked, ran across the room into the corner, and remained quiet. Otto and Maya both chuckled as if Otto was only playfully joking, but to Hedy it became a lifetime memory—a hurtful one. She couldn't help but notice how much in love they were with one another that they didn't seem to notice anyone else.

The following month Otto and Maya married and became an inseparable, strong unit. Otto formally adopted Hedy as his own child, and she took his name. Hedy was very happy that he'd adopted her, as it helped alleviate her fears, and she soon began feeling she belonged to a stable and loving family. He was strict, stern, and stoic in showing love, repetitively saying things like, "Never say the words 'I can't' and 'No excuses.'" In hindsight, Hedy said growing up with him was hard sometimes but it kept her "flying right," and she chose to hand down Otto's advice. The bottom line is that Otto brought stability to their lives. Maya was sometimes moody, so Otto felt keeping Maya happy was important in order to have a happy family. The love between the three of them was growing and Otto and Maya showed Hedy a loving relationship between parents, even though she did not see that at first as a child. They gave her a great example of devotion.

CHAPTER 4

THE HOLOCAUST AND THE WAR

People spent many nights huddled together in the small, deep cellars of their apartment buildings after the loud sirens warned of planes coming to bomb the town. Night after night, people had to come up with ways to keep their children and one another calm. Playing the harmonica, singing soft lullabies, and telling stories of better days soothed them for a time, but eventually they realized the war was not going to end anytime soon. Parents were forced to send their children to the countryside where the bombing was less severe. One way or another the children were sent on some kind of train far away from home. Together Otto and Maya hid several Jews and other people who refused to join the Nazi party inside their home, and also aided many in their escape. It seemed no one was safe in these times and you were arrested for just chewing gum the wrong way. They would hide under floorboards, in attics, in spaces behind the walls, and stay there until they could wait for the next move to get out of the country. Many countries are close to Germany, but it was difficult to get through the guarded borders. They risked their lives daily. The constant unexpected raids of the Nazis continued with more and more family and friends sent away. People didn't know whom to trust. It could be a friend or neighbor that reported "suspicious activity" in your home. They decided to send Hedy to the countryside where it was less dangerous than the city with buildings potentially crumbling all around.

Hedy had just begun feeling like part of a family and now she was going to have to be separated, not just from her mother, but from her father as well. She lay in bed night after night, thinking about how she would be leaving her parents to live with total strangers in the countryside until it was safe to return. *How long would that be?* She wondered. *What if my parents get killed?* She didn't know if she would ever see them again.

The day soon came, faster than Hedy wanted. She and her parents scurried to the train and they abruptly and quickly placed her in a seat by the window. Hedy remembers Maya putting a necklace around her neck, kissing her, and saying, "Be brave, and don't cry." She was taught that crying was a sign of weakness; not crying was a sign of strength and bravery. Hedy held back her tears out of respect, and watched through the train's filmy old window as it pulled away from the station, making loud clanking noises, while Maya and Otto remained standing and waving good-bye on the platform, as the train pulled farther and farther away. Soon Hedy could no longer see her parents from the window. Many people were being sent away and separated. Panic set into her heart and a lump went into her throat. She looked at her necklace, held it in her hand, closed her eyes, and drifted off to sleep.

Hedy arrived at a farm in the middle of the country. She remembers the people there as strange, angry, and busy. No greeting for her, as a large farm woman firmly grabbed her arm and pulled her in the direction of the old farmhouse she would be living in. No warm eyes, just frustrated, resentful, overworked, simple folks, who were forced to care for these strange city kids. "Well come on already, we don't have all day to waste" said the farm women. Children were seen as just another mouth to feed and an imposition. Hedy wandered anywhere she wanted, with no one checking on her, and spent days alone in the endless fields amongst the big-eyed, constantly chewing and drooling dairy cows. No one ever called her home for supper, or cared whether she washed her hair. Eventually the loneliness became unbearable and the animals became her friends. One day the farmers forced Hedy to watch as they slaughtered them for dinner. Hedy couldn't eat her pets, so she grew thin, eating greens and grains. She felt appreciative of the roof over her head; however, Hedy's thoughts continued to wonder what Maya and Otto were doing. She missed them every day.

One windy day, as a storm was approaching, Hedy lingered out in the fields. She was looking at the clouds and the wind blowing the grass and saw a little dog running toward her. The frightened dog jumped onto her, and Hedy held her shaking body in both arms. She befriended the lost little gray-and-white miniature schnauzer and named her Selma. They spent every day together from that day on, and Hedy watched squeamishly as Selma would dig up mice in the field for fun. At first Hedy screamed at the sight of the mice, but she eventually saw the way Selma liked them, so she started to like them as much as she could, and together they would play with them. The cows also roamed the fields often. Hedy referred to them as "those stupid cows" because one time a cow stepped on her foot when she got too close, and the big beefy cow did not budge for a long time. Her foot was swollen and she hobbled on it for weeks. Who knew how hard it was to make a cow move?

Meanwhile back in the city, Otto and Maya were in constant danger. They had no way of contacting Hedy, and they missed her very much. They had been struggling in the unsafe environment of war. Air raids every night, bombs dropping from the sky, explosions in places they never dreamed would be destroyed. Relatives were being sent away on trains never to be heard from again. Life was fragile and they had to run to safety almost daily. Otto refused to join the political Nazi party, but he was useful as an airplane mechanic, and he was needed to repair the fleets. Maya was once buried alive under the rubble of her bombed apartment for more than three days until she was found.

Hedy walked the large farm fields and wandered toward the woods one day, even though she wasn't supposed to, and entered the dark forest all alone. She stumbled upon an old shack, and saw a crumbling-looking chimney with smoke coming out. She approached cautiously, and soon saw a bunch of cats around the outside of the house. Inside lived Rosl and at least a hundred cats. Rosl welcomed Hedy inside her home and paid attention to her the way she wanted: hugs, smiles, warm compassion, and a cup of tea. She listened to Hedy's endless stories, and Hedy visited her day after day.

Rosl's eyes were radiant and loving, and she had an inviting energy that made Hedy comfortable. Having had no children of her own, she longed for them, but was beaten by her abusive, drunk of a husband and could not have them after he had hurt her so badly. He eventually left her, and she remained alone, shy, and afraid of people. But she was not afraid of Hedy. Here to her door came this lost little girl needing attention, and Rosl had her chance to give her every ounce of love she had ever stored up for a child, and she gave it all to Hedy.

Rosl wore traditional German dirndl clothes. A red kerchief in her long gray braided hair, she was missing patches of hair, overweight, and extremely poor. Her hands were calloused, and she had cat hair on just about everything. Despite the rundown condition of Rosl's home, however, Hedy could only see the love in her eyes, the reaching out of her worn hands, her kind voice, the goodness. These two lonely people spent many days together and became quite fond of each other. Hedy loved Rosl so much that she vowed if she ever had a daughter, she would make Rosl the godmother. She kept this promise, many years later. Rosl was my godmother.

When the war ended and Hedy returned to the city, she heard horror stories about the number of times her parents were buried alive when the house was bombed. She wasn't sure what to expect, but just gratefully relieved that her parents were still alive.

During the war they lived with very little, but they lived. They only ate half a potato a day because of food rations, so Hedy grew up malnourished to the point of randomly fainting alone in the streets as she grew thinner and thinner.

They made a real effort during these hard times to have small amounts of fun together despite their impoverished situation. They didn't have a television. The war's aftermath left so much death, poverty, and destruction. Survival came by being grateful for what they did have -- each other and their lives. So they sang all kinds of song together, silly ones, serious ones and sad ones. They played cards and silly games with spoons, made silly faces, and did silly dances as they laughed together.

Life got better slowly, and after the war was over, despite the ruins of destruction, and having their house bombed to the ground, they managed to recover. They rebuilt from nothing except Otto's drive of love for his family, and saved to get Hedy to college. She was going to be a pediatrician. He still kept saying, "Never say you can't" to the point where Hedy got sick of hearing those words. Hedy told me she probably would have been quite tough and wild to manage in her youth if it hadn't been for his stern hand of love. Otto who did come from a wealthy family lost everything because he continued to refuse to join the Nazis. They came to his home and asked him to join. When he refused they took it all away and executed some of the members of his family. Stories were passed around of his Uncle Philip being beheaded after being imprisoned first and then starved. He kept alive for a short time by eating garbage or spiders. Hedy said grateful and fondly of Otto, "He made me who I am today and I am thankful." When Hedy was a teenager, Maya and Otto deeply yearned to have a baby together. This was highly unlikely first because of the war and later after the war ended; their age limited their chances. .

CHAPTER 5

MAYA'S BABY GIRL

Otto and Maya tried after the war, but still never had their own child together. They kept getting told of their slim chances, so they were giving up more and more. In those days, women were considered past childbearing years at Maya's age, which were her late thirties. Then against the odds a blessing happened -- Maya was pregnant. By this point, Hedy was seventeen, the war had ended a few years before, and she was excited about having a baby brother or sister. A new day was dawning, with hope and happiness. Hedy had never seen Otto and Maya with so much light in their eyes, so full of joy and love. This was the happiest time in Maya and Otto's life together. They considered that baby a gift, a dream come true, finally their little miracle. The future arrival of this child brought some hope for them all. Imagining a birth after seeing all the death from war was restoring their small fragment of fragile faith. During the war they lost all belonging, and freedoms. They were not able to practice religion during the war, as they were told Hitler wanted the people to worship him. They began to focus on self-reliance and survival. This happy time of expecting a child changed them, brought them back to life, and created further inner healing of their hearts and souls. A new strength blossomed.

Life was taking hold again. Their hearts opened and began to feel joy. Otto catered even more to Maya, treated her delicately and carefully. He never let her bend, reach, or lift. He pampered her every day while she instinctively took the best care of herself and the unborn baby.

The day finally arrived and Maya went into labor. Otto drove her to the Catholic hospital. The nuns first made Maya comfortable by placing her in her bed. The nuns were very strict and would not allow her husband to be by her side. Soon after, Otto was asked to leave as per hospital policy of men not being able to witness the birth or stay the night. Late that night, Maya started having terrible labor pains and couldn't sleep, so the nuns gave her a strong sedative and told her the baby wouldn't be coming for hours yet. She continued to scream and cry in pain so they moved her down the long sterile hallway to the farthest room from the nurse's station. For the rest of the night, the nuns played cards at the nursing station. Maya could hear their voices in the distance until her eyes closed and she fell deeply asleep.

Early the next morning, when they went to check on Maya, she was lying in bed, in a pool of blood, hardly awake, almost unconscious. Her baby girl was born in the bed and she was holding her in her arms. Maya named her Andrea, but the cord was wrapped around her neck, and the cord strangled her. Cold and blue, Andrea only lived for minutes. She had an entangled scarf of her own. Maya said she had screamed for help in her loudest voice, but it was faint because she was too weary from the sedative. No one heard her, and no one came. She said she couldn't get the umbilical cord off Andrea's neck because it was too tight, entangled, and by the time she could loosen it the baby was gone. Her state of sedation caused blurry vision, poor motor control, and Maya went into shock bleeding. She had watched her baby be strangled until she took her last breath. Maya almost bled to death as well.

That was the day the light in Maya's glistening sparkling brown eyes went out, never to fully return. Otto came soon after he was notified. The once-strong vibrant man became so heartbroken and sobbed privately outside the room after seeing Maya and the baby. After they told Hedy the baby had died, they grieved. Otto and Maya grieved privately in their own way, and tried to be pleasant around one another, but it was just too painful to speak of openly. That was their last chance to have a baby, and they locked that pain tightly in a box inside their hearts forever. The loss of their baby also drove them farther away from God. They did not speak of faith, hope or religion. It was a dying ember in their hearts. The strangled child was buried along with much of the light within their spirits. Hedy felt the loss of her sister. She was heartbroken.

CHAPTER 6

THE STREET CAR

When Hedy was college age, she went off to school -- what she described as a castle -- to study to be a pediatrician. In time, she discovered she didn't like it, even though she did learn to speak seven languages. After she graduated, she chose to work for the railroad, and within a few years she had more than forty men working beneath her. Women holding high government or corporate positions was unusual in those days. Hedy was independent, but because she was left alone so much as a child, she liked living at home with Otto and Maya while she worked. She never got her own apartment, but she dated a rich, handsome man on and off for about seven years. They were engaged on and off, as well. It was just a crazy, yo-yo kind of relationship, with lots of passion and drama, which soon led to frustration and frequent arguments and break ups.

Then Hedy met Walter, a tall, dark, and handsome man, on a streetcar heading home from work late one night, and they decided to go on a date. Walter was a man who "fought for love," so after he and Hedy dated a few times, he told the other guys to "stay away from Hedy or I will make sure of it." Hedy admired Walter's direct actions, his powerful professions of love, but she let him know that she respected herself. One day, on a walk through the woods, Walter made a pass at Hedy, which she rejected by slapping him in the face, and Walter found himself walking home alone. He went off to the United States, and they exchanged one or two letters afterward.

One day when Hedy had a rare day off from work and decided to stay home, she peeked out the window to see if the mail had arrived. At that exact moment, Walter happened to be walking up the hill by her house and she saw him from her window on the third floor. She couldn't stop herself from shouting his name, "Walter!" He looked up to see who was calling him, their eyes met, and she came running to meet him. Time had passed and they had both matured. Soon after a courtship and an engagement, they were married.

Walter, who worked for Carl Zeiss, accepted a contract to work in the United States for two years. So he and Hedy packed their bags and off they went to the States on the Italian ship the Leonardo Da Vinci. They believed America was the land of opportunity where all the rich people lived. Hedy cried her eyes out because she had to leave her mother and father once again. She wondered why they were always being separated. She longed for her parents during the war and now she was moving across the ocean. This time Otto and Maya cried, too. Hedy consoled herself thinking it was a temporary stay. She thought she would return after two years. In the meantime, she vowed to write a letter to them every week.

The seas were rough on the *Leonardo Da Vinci,* and there was no dramamine available. Hedy had envisioned herself on a glamorous voyage but found she couldn't wear a single sequined ball gown she had packed. She was too busy turning pale shades of green, while hanging over the side of the ship vomiting into the deep blue ocean waves.

Eventually, however, she and Walter happily arrived in America and moved to an apartment in Brooklyn -- Prospect Park West.

They both rode the subway to work every day, as both worked for the same company. New York City was so much bigger than they were used to in Germany, but they were excited and homesick all at the same time. Hedy reminded herself over and over again that she would not be gone long from Otto, Maya, and the life she knew in Germany. After all, she had given up her government railroad job, and her pension, so that Walter could have this opportunity. Maya had photos of her daughter covering her mantle. Maya felt this was another separation.

CHAPTER 7

WALTER'S CHILDHOOD

Walter's parents were Ernst and Anna. Back in 1920, Walter's dad Ernst was a Medallion cab driver in New York City. He met his mother, a lawyer's governess. Mayor Mickey Walker married the two. When the depression hit, his parents returned to Germany. Walter was born in Ulm by the Danube River. The same birthplace as Albert Einstein. Walter was healthy and athletic, and had a bright mind, but his younger and only brother Manfred had asthma and was sickly. Manfred required his parents' constant attention, so they often left Walter alone when he was a child. Walter remembers evacuating their home all alone during the war when the bomb siren went off. Most of the time it went off during the night, and Anna and Ernst had to take turns to carry Manfred because he was so ill and too weak to run. Walter quietly kept a small suitcase with a few belongings under his bed, which he carried when he had to leave his home and run for safety. He remembers his mother running through the fire with falling beams while pulling him and carrying his brother to safety. Many times he would run alone and not be reunited with his family for days. He had to survive on his own in the streets amidst the fire, smoke and ashes of buildings burning to the ground. He sat alone in the rubble as a frightened boy, and watched the horrors of men and women screaming and dying in explosions. When the bombing stopped days later, he would have to find his way back home. To be safer, the family moved to Herlingen, an aunt's home in the country near the Blau River. There Walter attended school with Manfred Rommel four years older than he. Mrs. Rommel and her son lived in a large villa built by Russian prisoners. Walter remembers giving prisoners milk and bread on his way to deliver products to Mrs. Rommel. In turn, the prisoners gave Walter figurines they made.

Ernst had his own trucking business and was quite well off. The trucks at one time moved cement for the 1936 Olympic Stadium in Berlin. Hitler took Ernst's trucks during the war and the Nazi's made Ernst drive ammunition all through the war hoping he would get blown to pieces. Ernst was also a very smart man. Hitler was going to execute him for not joining the Nazi party, but he found him useful for a while, so he kept him alive. Ernst was a useful pilot and navigator amongst other things. He had flown with the Red Baron, Manfred Von Richthofen during WW1. We actually have a photo of Ernst and him standing together near their plane. Ernst was his chief navigator, and several very interesting stories have been passed down. One such story was the Red Baron developed a deep depression from so much killing during the war. It caused them great concern for his well being. Ernst was also a peaceful man, a worrier, and a late-night thinker. He could stay up all night thinking and worrying all by himself, smoking a cigarette, and sitting in a chair at the table, using a candle for light.

Anna was excellent in all the labors a woman traditionally did in those times. Anna was an amazing cook. Every Saturday night she baked an extraordinary cake, a real work of art. No one was allowed to touch it until Sunday, but Ernst would sneak up before Anna awoke on Sunday mornings and cut the cake straight down the middle, remove a straight middle slice, and push both sides of the cake back together again. Walter carried on this tradition with great joy, and Anna never let on that she noticed.

Walter traveled often after the war and later in life. He even stayed in a hut in the Amazon rainforest, surrounded by monkeys, walking on tree hanging walkways, researching many medicinal uses for plants, including a tree bark the natives used to cure indigestion. They also were searching for a cure for diabetes. He worked with researchers often and had interesting stories. Walter was intelligent and well read. He worked with lasers before they were publically used. He knew things about NASA and he fitted his company's camera in the astronauts' gloves before they went to the moon. We never knew all of Walter's secrets and accomplishments. He was very humble and private. I asked him once about the Mars rover in the Smithsonian, and he seemed to know the person who made it.

"Wow!" I said.

Humbly and honestly he replied, "Yes, but it's not a very good job."

"Why?" I asked.

"Because how many rovers do you need?" he said. "Once it is made you are out of a job."

I always loved his honest opinions.

Walter was as good a friend as he was a father, offering practical and realistic advice when asked. He treated people with respect and never talked down to a child. He could converse with anyone about anything and regularly told stories about the places he'd been. He talked to people as if he'd known them for a long time. He instilled confidence in me throughout my life. Above all, he was known for his sense of humor. He loved to laugh, even at his own stories and jokes.

Walter was also a wonderful husband and family man. He worked hard every day and came straight home. He was an amazing dancer. He strutted like a peacock, turning the heads of many ladies. Hedy never felt threatened by other ladies. She was graceful and confident in herself. It was a compliment to her, she would say.

Walter laughed and played with us children on the floor every night when he came home from work. He was a progressive man for the times, as he also helped clean the house. He and Hedy both worked and they were a team. Walter took care of us when she worked, and he had no problem helping his lady do the dishes when she let him.

Walter told many tales of American Indians and grizzly bears from when he was a young lumberjack in Canada. In fact, we heard a bedtime story about grizzly bears every night. One of them even took his lunchbox! He appreciated the American Indians' love of the earth and their connection to animals, which our family came to enjoy. Walter shared with us that Indians believe animals have spirits. That's how we connect with them along with every other living thing on earth. They believe nature is important, and in it, we are all connected with one another. They also use the natural medicines the earth provides to cure as well as prevent illnesses.

Walter told very few stories of the war, however. When the war ended, it seemed as if he thought it was best to move forward and not bring up what we cannot change. We knew it greatly affected him, but it gave him an appreciation for life, family, adventure, freedom, and America.

CHAPTER 8

HEDY AND WALTER'S BABY GIRL AND BABY BOY

They were young and beautiful, and soon the two years flew by. They experienced New York City, made friends, and took great pride in studying to become American citizens. When they got their citizenship, they felt very proud and accomplished. From that day forward, anytime someone asked about their nationality, they spoke of themselves as Americans first. Then came Hedy's deep desire to start a family of her own. Walter didn't really want children yet, but he loved Hedy so much he couldn't say no. They tried and tried, but because Hedy was so malnourished during the war that her reproductive organs did not develop properly and doctors told her it was unlikely she would ever conceive. But Hedy, being a warrior, refused to give up and met a wonderful doctor who helped her achieve her dream of having a baby.

That's how my life began; I was born the first American descendent. I was a lovely breech birth, sitting upright in the womb, trying to jump feet first into the world. Mom was scared because there was a big thunder and lightning storm that night. Plus the wallpaper in the hospital room had angels on it. Anything religious reminded her of Maya losing Andrea at birth in the Catholic hospital. She would actually shudder at angels and say they reminded her of death, and she wanted death to be far, far away and unknown. She never talked about it; she had seen enough death in her life. "Let's live and celebrate life," she would say.

Maya and Otto never forgave the nuns for not checking on Maya that night. They had lost their little girl. Consequently, they stayed away from churches, any church.

Doctors didn't let men in the room when their wives were giving birth, so Walter had to leave during the thunderstorm when Hedy went into labor. She was scared to be alone after what happened to Maya, and he didn't want to leave her. So he waited excitedly at a nearby restaurant and gave out cigars. Men lived it up while women gave birth.

When the baby was being born, Hedy remembers the lights flickering on and off during the thunderstorm. Thunder and lightning lit up the angels on the wallpaper, which freaked her out. She thought she might die. The doctor finally came into the room and said the baby was breech and had to be turned, so he stuck his arm up her vagina to turn me. She worried that the cord was around my neck, and sure enough, the doctor said it was. It brought back memories of that terrible tragedy of Maya's baby girl being strangled. The possibility of loosing another baby to a strangulating cord was overwhelming and Hedy began to panic. Her trust and faith in hospitals and doctors was shaken as well as her faith. The doctor worked himself into a sweat, and then told her he felt very lucky that he was able to turn the baby and get the tightly wrapped cord from around her neck before it strangled her. It was a close call, but I was born healthy.

My mom held me like I was the best treasure in the world, a dream come true, a gift and a blessing. She was so excited to be a mother and have a family. All was a celebration of my amazing arrival, and Walter was enamored with us both. Plus Maya and Otto had a granddaughter. Although the scars remained and hardened the hearts, their hearts began to heal again. The arrival of the baby girl brought them closer and able to warm the embers of their hearts. They were cautious not to get too happy after all they had been happy before and watched things slip away. They eventually made the choice to put it all behind them, and decided to once again to build a life that they wanted.

When I was two years old, Walter and Hedy decided we needed a house, a backyard, and a white picket fence. So we moved from Brooklyn, New York, to Union, New Jersey, into a cape cod that we painted canary yellow. My dad built us a white picket fence and lined the trellis over the gate with red, pink, white, and yellow, rose bushes. It was our very own picture-perfect dream home. Walter took the bus to New York City for work, and within a year they bought a car, an Opal, which is my birthstone, even though that's not the reason they bought the car. Soon after Robert was born and they now had their beautiful baby boy and I had a beautiful baby brother.

Hedy got her figure back soon after having the baby, and it was most important to her. She looked just like a supermodel, tall, all legs, and not an ounce of fat on her. She took driving lessons in her orange jumpsuit and black fur hat, always showing off every curve of her figure. She liked being beautiful; I thought she looked like a movie star.

Robert was beautiful. He had the cutest chubby legs, and was the apple of all our eyes. He was a calm and peaceful baby. When he arrived it was such a blessing. He was my baby brother, and a baby doll to play with and help my mom. He brought me high hopes for being a friend and playmate in the future. I looked forward to spending time with him.

Life was calm and stable. Our family seemed complete. It was now shifting from loosing people to growing. We often did long to be together with our family still separated by the seas.

My mother was careful not to let us out of her sight. She played with us and spent her time with Robert and I, smiling and loving us. I went to kindergarten when I was four and was worried I would miss my mother. I was born after the enrollment date cut-off, but they took me early after meeting me and testing me. I found friends in kindergarten that made me look forward to going. People can be that for you sometimes. They can be the reason you get through difficult times and brighten your life.

Many times later in life when Hedy missed me or felt alone, she would remember my words the day before kindergarten. She tells the story with such a deep feeling of comfort. She said I placed my little hand on her check as I sat in her lap. She always said that little hand on her check felt so warm, soft, and sincere. The words I spoke affected her all her life: "I will never leave you, Mommy; I promise." She was so surprised and happy to hear that because she felt alone a lot when she was a child, so when I said that to her she felt as if I meant "forever." Looking into my eyes, she saw a promise that was more than a little girl's words. I meant what I said. I always came back. I knew instinctively that my family had separation issues from the wars aftermath and I tried to comfort my mother.

I grew up speaking both German (until I was four) and English. I spoke English in kindergarten, and we went to school a half day. It was hard to be away from my mom, but I made a few new friends and sat next to a nice boy named Steven who comforted me when I missed my mom. She knitted my skirts, and dressed me so neatly. I wrote songs for her and sang them, and made her bouquets of any kind of flower I could find that was pretty, like daisies and dandelions. She said I always made her so happy.

Life in the suburbs consisted of putting on backyard plays, mermaid shows in our above-ground pool, and building tree houses. Our generation played outside. We didn't have a television at first. When we finally got one, we were only allowed to watch it for an hour during Saturday-morning cartoons. My mother didn't allow for what she called "too much mindless time in front of that box." Internet and cell phones hadn't been invented yet either. We rode bicycles, played hopscotch, bounced balls, went on treasure hunts, played with our pet rabbits, played dress-up, and went on picnics.

I always liked putting on shows in my yard with my brother and all the neighborhood kids to raise money for UNICEF. I wrote and begged my uncle Manfred who now lived in Australia to send me a Koala Bear for the circus portion of the show, but I never got one. Manfred was a bushman, a type of Crocodile Dundee, who lived in the outback of Australia. He lived in a house he built alone that was solar powered before solar power was en vogue, and mined for opals. He left a corporate high-paying job for the freedom to do what he wanted. He once sold his opals, bought a motorcycle and traveled the world. He did not like living "a cookie cutter pattern like everyone else," he would say.

CHAPTER 9

TRIPS TO AMSTERDAM AND GERMANY

Walter became a very good soccer player in Germany. When he lived in the USA he played on weekends at Farcher's Grove, a German soccer field and Hoffbrau. After the games, German musicians and dancers were featured under a pavilion. He reconnected with an old soccer buddy named Walter Schumacher, who happened to immigrate to America, too. Walter S. had some connection to Pele and the Cosmos, which was the first professional soccer team in the United States.

On weekends, we visited Walter S. and his wife Carla. We all sat outside at the picnic table, talking about sports. Carla was a widow and had two sons from a previous marriage. Walter S. was a widower with one son. By the time he and Carla found each other and got married, their sons were already adults living away from home. So they loved to travel together. We all became such good friends that when I was nine years old, Walter and Carla invited me to join them on a trip to Holland/Amsterdam and Germany. I was so excited, especially since I got to stay with Otto and Maya in Germany! We flew on KLM, and one of the stewardesses gave me a wing-shaped pin because I was so brave to be going away from my mommy and daddy by myself. My mom was so nervous. She was as protective as a lioness she even paced like one.

Off to Amsterdam we flew. Unfortunately the flight with them was so boring and uncomfortable because even though Walter S. and Carla weren't beyond their forties, they didn't have any young children, so they seemed old. They acted old. I was looking forward to meeting Maya, Otto, and Rosl after stopping a few days in Amsterdam.

A big storm rocked the plane. People screamed and the oxygen masks came down, but I slept through the whole thing. When we landed, a stewardess woke me and I threw up all over Carla. The stewardess helped her clean up in the bathroom, and she changed her clothes after we got our luggage at the airport. Then the car came to take us to Carla's friends' house in Holland where we were staying. They owned a major bicycle chain. I spoke no Dutch, so I had no one to talk to but Walter S. and Carla.

When we arrived a maid asked me what I wanted to eat. I knew she was a maid because she wore a white apron over a black dress every day, the house we stayed in had cherry red carpeting, and she walked fast up the stairs, carrying a shiny silver tray. When it was time to eat, she brought the tray to my room. I always picked strawberries and whipped cream from the menu because I wasn't sure what the other foods were. For some reason, I thought goats were on the menu. The milk was warm goat's milk. I wasn't used to that.

One day while I was riding a bicycle I noticed a boy about my age sitting on the grass by the side of the road, and his bike lying next to him on the ground. I circled a around him and pulled over. He had sandy brown/blond hair, a square face and haircut, and he wore plaid shorts.

"Are you ok?" I asked.

He looked at me strangely because I was speaking English, but he understood me. He smiled and said, "Yes," and then said his name was Oscar. Oscar didn't know much English but we managed to communicate well enough and both of us had fun learning new words from one another. We rode our bikes alongside one another and he showed me beautiful fields of never-ending red tulips. I asked him whether people really wore wooden shoes there. He smiled and showed me a small local shop where I could get a pair to bring home. They were wooden all right, with a picture of a windmill painted on them. I wore them, though nobody else did, and they hurt my feet almost right away.

We played daily, rode to parks, and picked red tulips. Having a new friend to share the day with was so much fun. He was the best part of the trip there.

My uncle Walter S., as I had been calling him since the trip, kept trying to take photos of me when we were at the house or going to the movies or somewhere touristy, and I would run and hide behind a tree and stick my tongue out. I felt awkward having my picture taken. I just wanted to play. He got angry, but I didn't care; I didn't like pictures taken of me at that age. He was persistent and annoying about it. At first he said he would tell my parents if I didn't cooperate, but he gave up eventually. He showed my parents the film of me sticking my tongue out at him. My parents just laughed.

We left for Germany and Carla didn't want to sit next to me this time, so she and Walter S. both sat behind me, and I got an aisle seat. The flight from Amsterdam to Germany was much shorter than the one from the States to Amsterdam, and we soon landed in Germany without any problems.

The airport in Holland looked more bright and colorful than the airport in Germany, which carried a color scheme of gray, beige, and sparkling clean. It also had more people in it than the airport in Holland; it was busier and city-like. German was just more formal, as I could sense the culture of discipline and organization. It was like a well-oiled machine.

Then came the car, a big Mercedes Benz in an eggshell finish. My little round Omi Maya and my Opa Otto got out. They were focused on me like a football in the middle of a pileup. They zoomed toward me protectively, gave me a quick hug, and then we got right into the car. I loved the way the doors closed so quiet and tight.

United we went to their apartment on the third floor in the city of Stuttgart. It was the same one Hedy grew up in after the war. The town looked alpine with geraniums hanging out the windows and cobblestone streets. It had a bakery we could walk to and outdoor shops and markets that sold bread, fruit, and all kinds of foods. We parked and got out of the car, and I took in every bit of ambiance, as I imagined my mom living there while she was growing up. I felt it would have been nicer if we all were together, maybe someday.

When we got to the third floor, we opened the door and I could feel my mom's home. How amazing it was to get a peek at her childhood home with her parents. I felt as if I was home, too. Her old room was kept the same, they said. She had black wallpaper with white lotus flowers on the walls. In Hebrew, my name Susanne means "lily," and a lotus is a type of lily. Names do carry interesting meanings. An antique armoire was standing tall in the corner and it had a skeleton key. With a giggle and impatiently jumping in place, Maya told me to open it. It was full of marzipan and chocolate-covered marshmallows with a cookie on the bottom. I had enough goodies for a year. This trip was starting off deliciously.

The furniture in the house was antique. When I described it to Hedy, she said she never liked anything antique at our house in Union. She always bought modern stuff because she felt old things were too close to death. She seriously wanted nothing to do with memories of death and she made sure she lived young and modern. But I liked Maya's antique furniture and especially the skeleton key.

In the Germany apartment, we stood on a bath mat and bathed daily on a rigid schedule at the sink. There was no shower available.

We went for walks in the woods; they had a playful word we used for our walks in the woods. It was so much fun. Maya showed me a lot of edible things in the forest. Picking leaves and tasting them was fun. One leaf tasted like lemon and she said it was good to help cure thirst when you had no water to drink. She even knew all the right mushrooms to eat. She seemed like an old shaman woman at times. Both my grandparents and my mom were always strangely concerned about whether I had a bowel movement daily. The way they worried about constipation was too funny. I figured it must be something you worry about when you get older.

We went sightseeing in Otto's big Mercedes. He got a new one of his choice every year as a benefit from his high position at Mercedes Benz until he retired. Upon his retirement, the company gave him a medal called the Blue Max. It was an honor and also demonstrated loyalty and longevity with the company. He also belonged to a private country club. It had water fountains and a park, complete with volleyball, picnics, sandboxes, and a swimming pool. I wanted to go there every day. One day I met a boy and a girl in the sandbox, and they were excited to meet someone from the United States. They asked me if I could give them something said that said "USA" on it. I jokingly told them that my underwear says "USA" on the back, and gave it to them. They were so excited they ran around with it. My grandpa Otto was watching me as he lit up his cigar by the clubhouse. He politely but very sternly said, "Don't do that again."

"It was clean," I replied. He tried hard not to laugh and remain stern, but his eyes smiled. The children at the park gave me a pair of socks that had a German emblem on them. We went to that country club day after day. Some days we went to castles and famous gardens, but when my grandparents asked me where I wanted to go, I always said "the Galende." They smiled each time and off we went, so happy and relaxed. I loved being with them so much. We were crazy, absolutely crazy about each other, as if we had known each other all our lives. I wished for us all to be together. I went to bed tired every night from the day's adventures. Then one night I went to bed excited and it was difficult to sleep for the next day I would meet my Tante Rosl in person for the first time. It seemed like the day just couldn't come fast enough. I would awake through the night and open my eyes only to see the darkness fill the room. Finally I awoke to a faint but warm golden sunlight peering in through the window of my mother's childhood bedroom.

The special, long-awaited day came, the day I was to meet Rosl in person and spend the day with her, just as she promised. Rosl was a comfort to Hedy when she was separated from her parents and living with strangers in the countryside. Rosl drove all the way into the city to pick me up. Driving to the city was something Rosl never liked to do; it was very frightening to her.

Unfortunately, Maya did not like her very much and routinely rolled her eyes as she remarked how dirty and unkempt Rosl was. Nonetheless, Rosl drove to Maya's home and I came down from the third floor to meet her . She drove a very old dark grey Volvo. Rosl fit Hedy's description perfectly as she reminded me of a Hansel and Gretel character. She wore a kerchief and dress with an apron, and lived in the woods. I had not seen a photo of her before, but we did have one. Most of the photos Maya had were destroyed in the war. Bombs destroyed Hedy and Walters baby pictures. All was lost and burned. Material things came and went; only love lasted. That was the lesson from the war. Time spent with one another mattered more than anything. Life was precious, and time was not guaranteed.

Rosl never had children, but Mom made her my godmother. It was funny, my parents did many of the main things for religion, but I never really heard them speak of Jesus, Angels, or God. I really didn't know what a godmother even meant. I was told it was someone special to look out for me and it was considered an honor.

As I got in Rosl's car, Maya turned her back and barely even said hello. Rosl's car was filled to the windows with things, like a hoarder, and coated in cat hair. She liked animals better than most people. She had brown hair with a patch missing in the front and a face that was puffy and weathered.

But her eyes sparkled like small diamonds. Her smile was like a girl in a candy shop. When she saw me, she could barely hold back the tears. I could feel all the love she had and I cried plenty of tears myself. "Quickly," she said, "let me look at you with my old eyes. Ah, Hedy's daughter." Then we wiped our tears with her old handkerchief, and she said robustly that she had waited so long for that day. Clearing her throat she continued, "We are not crying; we are going shopping." She wanted to buy me the best dress at the best shop! She had an old rag with many coins in it and some paper money she kept in a jar. She said she had never been to a fancy store in her life, but she wanted to see one, in the big city, and see me wearing a dress from it, from her, any dress I wanted.

We arrived at the shop. It was a large building with big glass doors in front. There were gentlemen in front of the door with gold buttoned uniforms and hats. They opened the door for Rosl and me. I looked back to see the doorman giving Rosl a look of disgust as she walked in.

We went up the escalators to the top floor where the best dresses were. I really didn't care that much about a dress, but Rosl did and she mattered so much to me. I knew this was a once-in-a-lifetime day, maybe the first and last time we would ever see each other, so I was watching her, etching her voice, face, and movement in my heart. She wore a kerchief to hide from the stares of all the well-dressed people in the store. I said I liked everything she picked up to show me. I was trying to look for something inexpensive after seeing how big hearted she was and after seeing her jar. When she had her back turned I found a dress on the sale rack. She didn't want me to pick a dress from there, but I put the dress on one of the racks with the expensive dresses on it when she wasn't looking. Then we went through the rack, and I picked it out, a blue-grey dress with two heart-shaped buttons. It looked like a jumper over a shirt. I made a huge fuss over it and said I had to buy it. She was so excited that I had taken a dress off that rack. We went to the register, feeling very accomplished. Rosl was so proud. It gave her joy to see me happy and to show how important I was to her. I had the biggest smile as I watched her back because when the salesperson rang the dress up on the register, Rosl got ready to take out her bundle of coins and she looked up and said, "Wait a minute; what did you say?"

The salesperson repeated the price.

"Are you sure this is from the expensive rack?" she asked.

"Yes," said the salesperson.

"Then why does it cost so little?" she asked.

The salesperson replied, "I can charge more if you like."

Rosl was confused but I was happy and insisted that was the only dress I liked. I was worried she was onto me, but I was careful not to insult her and blow her joy. She quickly realized I did not understand the currency there, "the mark"; I only knew the dollar, but she snapped out of her puzzled look and trusted it. She and I hugged. I kept that dress like it was the cat's meow. My aunt Rosl had such a good heart.

She didn't want to keep me too long from my grandma, so she drove me home and apologized to me for my grandma's behavior. "Don't be angry with her," she said. "Just enjoy your time with her." She said we had the most beautiful moment that day, and moments can never be taken away. Then she hugged me with an everlasting hug and drove away. We decided we would not say the word "goodbye." Instead, we chose to say, "I love you."

Maya was outside before we even got back. She was curt and rude and commanded me to "Come on now" after I'd barely gotten out of the car and watched Rosl drive off. Maya rushed me back into the apartment as if she wanted to brush off the day. She didn't look at or comment on the dress much, just a quick "umm hmmm." Then we ate dinner. We washed up again at the sink, just as we did twice a day, and changed into our pajamas. Then she would brush my hair a hundred times every night before going to bed. She loved brushing my long wavy brown hair just like my moms. Otto watched, silently smoking his cigar in his chair next to us, feeling fortunate to have his girls next to him.

CHAPTER 10

MEANINGFUL VISITS WITH GRANDPARENTS

One night Maya came into my room to chat before I went to sleep. I had lots of questions about my mommy, her, and Otto. She loved telling me stories and we always giggled and snuggled until I fell asleep. We had a quiet moment that night and she was lying so close to me that our bodies were touching. She had been stroking my hair. I said to her, "Maya, didn't you and Otto ever want another baby?"

She said, "Why do you ask?"

I said, "I don't know. I just think you two are such good parents; that's all."

She said, "No, we have your mom and now you, so we are very happy."

I said, "Well, Maya, if it's okay, could you please call me Andrea tonight? Just call me Andrea."

Silence fell, her body stiffened up, and she set up on her elbow from her pillow.

"What did you say?" The air seemed to turn to ice.

"I said call me Andrea."

She paused and stared at me. Then Maya turned to the doorway and shouted for Otto. He came to the room. But when he got to the doorway she said "Never mind."

She was obviously shocked, and gave me a funny look. Then she said, "Susanne, I had a baby who died, and her name was Andrea, and your Opa and I can never speak that name because it hurts too much. I don't know why you say this name to me now, but please know we do not talk about it, okay?" She proceeded to sigh deeply and said, " I don't know how you knew that name." She wrote my mother a letter and my mother was horrified. My mother never told me that name, or about her baby sister that died. There are so many connections and mysteries in life.

"Okay," I said.

That was the first time I had ever heard of the baby girl named Andrea. That night, Maya stayed in my room and while lying in bed next to me she held me very closely. It was beautiful. Strangely the incident bonded us beyond words. It was like I awakened something inside both Maya and Otto. . Although we couldn't explain this event it was most unforgettable and chills went up our spines each time we thought of it. I always loved the name Andrea and felt so strongly drawn to it.

Within the next few days I had the opportunity to visit with my Omi Anna. She was patiently waiting to see when I would be able to visit when I arrived in Germany. I had met her when she visited the States. She had no daughter of her own and but did have two sons, and I was her only granddaughter as well. Maya told her I could only come for an afternoon, and they would pick me up and take me to their home. Anna did not have a car so Otto and Maya drove me to her home in the countryside. It seemed Maya was a little possessive and jealous every time I went to visit with someone else. Maya asked, "Do you really want to go, or we can go sight seeing? " I answered softly " I think I should go, we promised her." We drove silently as we came nearer to Anna's house Her house sat in the green rolling hills of the countryside, and looked like a Swiss chalet with red geraniums in the window boxes.

On the way there, I imagined what Walter's home would look like and how Anna would receive me in her home and what would we talk about.

When we pulled up to her house, I could feel butterflies in my stomach. I bravely shut the silent door of the light-colored car and walked up the hill of her drive. She was not outside her house and the door was closed, so we rang the door bell. No answer. *Did she forget ? Is she okay?* I wondered. We hollered her name. Shortly thereafter, she came to a window and waved us in. When I went inside, she called me to take my shoes off and come upstairs. "No street germs in the house from the bottom of your shoes," she would say.

After taking the last steep stair of a narrow white immaculate hallway, I grew slightly out of breath, and when I turned the corner, there she was, Anna, sitting in a chair by the kitchen table and near the window with a sunbeam that shined on her full head of white hair, not silver, but pure snowflake white. Her smile shined along with the sunbeam. Her face was shaped just like Walter's and mine, round full cheeks and almost no wrinkles. She had a slim ski-sloped nose, and she was about 5'5" with a mature but curvy figure.

Anna opened her arms and nodded for me to come into them. So I went quickly. She held me a moment and then said, "Let me look at you." She began to analyze my hair, feeling its texture between her two fingers, rubbing them back and forth, while looking at its color. Disappointed, she said, "Ah your hair is not fine; it is curly." I didn't know why that was disappointing. She then said "Just like your father's, but his fell out." She smiled the same smile Walter does, and both of them had eyes that squinted almost closed when their cheeks went up.

Then she broke the ice and began laughing, "Does your dad still use all those hair creams to make his hair grow?" That started the conversation easily and the laughter was almost constant. We always teased Dad about his hair vanity.

Soon the cuckoo came out of the clock and shouted its cuckoo bird call and we knew our time together was ending. We stood in the stream of light from the kitchen, and held unbroken eye contact silently for a long moment as if to take in everything about one another. We didn't get together often and we never knew when would be the last time we'd see each other.

With a great smile and a "holding back tears" hug, we decided not to make a scene. It was very hard to say goodbye and began to hurt my heart and stomach. I hated saying goodbye to her. We both became awkward, stumbling, and our movement reflected discomfort.

Maya and Otto were at the door soon after the cuckoo clock sang. Maya sure was prompt and eager to get me back with her and Otto. Anna said, "Go along now, and tell everyone back home hello and I love them; tell your dad." I slowly went down the stairs and then quicker toward the bottom. When I saw Otto and Maya I felt better.

We drove from the house and I was silent, just staring at her house, using my eyes to take a picture to last a lifetime. I wish I could have met Ernst, but he had passed away many years before. Next I began thinking about why she didn't come to the door when we arrived or when we left. Come to think of it, I only saw her stand up from her chair and sit back down. She did not move from the chair the whole time I was there. I never saw her walk!

Then I remembered those large ankles and weird-looking shoes that I never really saw except on elderly people and pondered whether she could walk well. In denial, my thoughts shifted to, *That couldn't be the reason, not with such a radiant smile, a great laugh, and a strong hug.* Then I paused to realize it was the reason and it made me sad to think she couldn't walk well. Then I further realized that she didn't want me to know she had a hard time walking or she would have told me. She tried to spare me her troubles, and in that I was sad but began to feel a strange love, as well. She loved me. I'd had a most amazing day. I tried to capture her hugs and the light from her smile and eyes into my body so I could never forget how she made me feel. I was afraid I would forget, but I still remember today.

CHAPTER 11

THE MOUNTAIN HOME

The next few years we spent some time doing new things, like going to the Poconos and looking at land on the weekends. Once we got a free microwave, just for coming to look at the land. Microwave ovens were the new way of cooking, and when we brought ours home and set it up, we paused and realized we were scared to death of it. "It cooks from the inside out with waves?" It was like something out of a science fiction movie. One time we got a sunfish sailboat. I got to pick the color so I picked red.

My mom and dad bought a piece of land and a home to live in, in Wild Acre Lakes, a community with five lakes and two pools. Boating, swimming, and a ski clubhouse were included. Walter had six weeks per year of vacation time from his company. We liked hiking, biking, and picking blueberries in the woods. My dad didn't like crowds of people and it was a nice getaway from the city.

Maya and Otto really enjoyed my visit to Germany and were missing me terribly. How come we are all always separated somehow? Soon after a few long-distance phone calls and letters, they decided they wanted to make a big life event by moving to the United States. Hedy and Walter excitedly told them they could build a home on the land they'd bought. They'd be an hour away and we could visit them on weekends and summers. Hedy would now have her mom, who she always missed in childhood, and the whole family together. What a dream come true. Hedy did whatever it took to make this dream happen.

Soon Hedy began working nights, and with passion, helped order materials and saw to it that the house in the mountains would be built to my perfectionistic Grandpa Otto's ways. He took forever to paint an Easter egg. Using oil paints, he painted the most beautiful mountain scenes on them. This man was a perfectionist in everything he touched: patient, pensive, and precise. He was the research and test engineer for Mercedes Benz and it showed in his everyday life.

Well, a united family was about to happen and Hedy was in full gear. Otto and Maya bought life insurance and gave up a lot of benefits in Germany, as the benefits in the United States were more expensive and covered far fewer services. Plus they barely spoke English. They knew how to say "yes" and "no" and that was about it. Moving to the States was a big adjustment at their age.

So, happily they came. They were a bit shy and standoffish, and stayed out of the house for a few weeks until it was completed enough to live in. I baked them a lemon cake with frosting for their arrival. Maya said, 'No thank you it looks much to sweet for me." I was perplexed. Otto put every nail in that house; he enjoyed building it. They never had their own free standing home before. He and Maya maintained a strict German household, clean and organized. No one was allowed to come into the house with his or her shoes on. I had to polish my bike on the weekends, and we ate hot soup for lunch in the summer. Otto made toast; he thought toasters were weird and didn't like the way margarine melted on it, so he would wait until the toast cooled before eating it.

We played cards together and silly Maya would take out her teeth and make us all laugh. We still weren't watching that much television. We were always busy outdoors. When we were inside we played board games and card games, did chores, read books. We collected rainwater outside in buckets and washed our hair in it, and we made our own perfume by putting lilac blooms inside little bottles. I kept toads and salamanders I found walking in the woods on rainy days. Maya made jars of things that would heal whatever ailed us. Sometimes we drank them, sometimes we smeared them on, and sometimes we soaked in them.

In the summertime I joined a swim team and played on a volleyball team with Hedy and Maya. It was like the war never happened. Robert was always riding his bike; he loved the outdoors. I was a dedicated competitive swimmer and won my races every year. One year my swim coach entered me in a beauty contest called Little Miss Wild Acres. She desperately wanted me to beat the girl who had won the previous year because she thought she was stuck up. "I beg you to win" my swim coach said. Joan's mom spent all year keeping her daughter out of the sun to avoid sunburn and to prepare for the contest. She made her the best costume, made sure she had no bruises or flaws, and kept her like a doll. Joan complained about her mom being too pushy because she forced her into the contest. I personally thought her mom was an overbearing, nervous lady. I felt sorry for Joan because she hadn't been allowed to play softball with me because she might have gotten dirty or injured. Well, I had an old gym mat and made up a gymnastics routine and to "Surfin' USA" by the Beach Boys. I didn't really understand what the big deal was, but I listened to my swim coach.

When the day came, Dad drove the gym mat to the clubhouse in the old station wagon with wood paneling on the sides. He and Mom both watched the pageant. Otto and Maya just sat like logs on the couch, as Otto totally disapproved of beauty contests and was disappointed in my mom because she let someone judge her daughter that way. He did not believe that beauty was an accomplishment. He believed we are born with our looks, so we can't take credit for them. Then why should we show them off? He also believed we shouldn't let others' opinions of us decide how beautiful we are. So they totally ignored us as we left for the clubhouse all excited. They didn't say a word, even after I won. I came home to silence and no eye contact, as if I were invisible.

Otto had seen pictures of Hedy in town when she was younger, wearing a ski outfit. A photographer took pictures of her and hung them in the big picture window of the photography shop in the center of town. Otto went to that shop, had them removed, and made Hedy give the money back. It was a matter of principle to him; he believed true achievement came with skill, hard work, and discipline.

Later after the summer ended, and the winter air chilled the mountain home, we heated one room with a stove and Maya sealed the heat in by hanging blankets in the doorway. They were very frugal and didn't like to waste anything. They felt heating the whole house was wasteful when we really only used one great room. We slept cold and under featherbed blankets. We had no heat in the bedrooms; it was so cold we could see our breath, but we were together.

CHAPTER 12

THE TRIP TO A PLACE WHILE IN HIS ARMS, WHICH I CALL HEAVEN

Snow was on the branches of the evergreen trees and the birch trees. I was alone with my head against the tow rope booth and my left cheek to the ground. I couldn't feel anything in my body. I heard someone moving toward me. It was a human figure in a white robe and light all around him. At first I thought it was my Dad. There were two others behind him I thought might be my mom and grandmother. But these most beautiful hands palms up reached toward me and held me. I understood in that moment it was Jesus himself. Even if I had known nothing about Him, I knew everything I needed to know when I met Him. It was as if every piece of information about Him was just transferred into my brain and heart right away from His hands. His hands were amazing and made me feel amazing. There was a calm and a comfort that is hard to find the words for. I felt no fear; He was like the most loving parent multiplied by a thousand. The hardest thing is to find the words for something that is so amazing. It was so remarkable that to this day there has not been a single experience that could ever compare.

There He was, kneeling in front of me while I lay by the booth. He did not look holographic or strange, just like a person with a loving energy glowing as bright as the sun and the size of Mount Everest. His love is so much more captivating than His physical appearance, though He was wearing white clothing and had long and wavy brown hair and hazel or light brown eyes. The physical did not matter any more. I began to focus on an inner beauty I saw to be more beautiful than any physical appearance. It was an aura that seemed to express what He was thinking and feeling. His physical features became very secondary to the love that He radiated.

His eyes and hands streamed love and connection that felt completely safe. His hands…His loving hands, palms up, reached for my being. As I began to anticipate how they would feel, they were already holding me to complete the feeling and made me smile through and through. His hands connected with every cell in my body and made me feel as if a quivering inpouring of excitement and energy was entering me. My mind, body, and spirit awakened in a sense of consciousness that I had never felt before in the most calm and intensely nourishing process. It was as if every part of me that felt worn out, tired, or simply as if I needed something, was filled. I was healed in places I didn't even know I needed healing. There was a beautiful light all around but I could still see the scenery around me. I heard and felt the message at the same time, "Don't be afraid; I am with you." It was so intense and it filled me so fast I had no time to be frightened. The physical features of Jesus faded, however, as I focused on His inner beauty, which radiated all around the other Heavenly beings. I believe He greatly loves children. He did everything to make me comfortable. I believe from this experience, He knew how and when to greet me in the way that was perfect for me to feel safe.

Two male angels appeared in the background. I didn't know what they were at first. I had never really thought about angels.

They just looked like large humans. A spirited safeness and trust overwhelmed my senses. I called them angels. They looked like you could crawl in their wings and rest in them like the safest, softest bed.

They were lighthearted and joyful, and their wings seemed natural for them. The wings were heavy and made a soft rustling sound when they walked. They looked like long grey-white feathers that blended in with the colors of winter. The angels were dressed like warriors and yet looked so compassionate. They were larger than humans, maybe ten feet tall, and their bulky wings arching slightly higher than their heads and extending down to their ankles. They looked rugged and muscular. One angel was smaller than the other, and it looked as if the smaller angel had his work cut out for him. His work boot laces were untied as he sauntered over being careful not to trip over his untied laces. It made me feel like giggling a little. Their chests were covered in some kind of heavy material, and they wore brown clothing over their chest. They had heavy footsteps.

As they approached me, the larger one turned back to the smaller one and told him to "hurry up." Both of them smiled and communicated that they were my friends and guides. They looked so strong. I did not see colorful bright female angels like in the picture books, but these guys were here for me.

Both angels were definitely part of a system under the direction of Jesus and worked with Him as a team. In that moment I realized again that all things and all beings are connected, and the word "lonely" was no longer needed. People are connected here in families and there is connection in spiritual as well. It is everywhere I soon awakened to realize; there is love all around us.

The angels communicated with one other without words but I understood them in my language. They said, "We have to take her now." I strongly sensed urgency.

Turning to me, Jesus said, "I'm here for you. You are safe now. We will take care of you, and will take you home, okay?"

"Okay," I answered.

The look of compassion was comforting; I had this overflowing feeling of peace and trust, as He was really there. I just let go and let myself trust and had faith that whatever He wanted for me was good. I didn't even question what was happening, and I question pretty much everything. What an amazing feeling to let go and trust. Being held and carried in Jesus's arms was my Heaven.

When we lifted up together and got off the ground higher above the hill, I heard a horrible cry (or scream) to the right, below me, and I was startled out of my serenity. I looked down. There at the bottom of the hill I saw my mother running around in circles like a chicken with her head cut off, holding her hands on top of her head, then moving them to her stomach and screaming a horrible scream. There she was in her pink winter coat, belted at the waist, and white fur on her hood. I panicked. Then I said, "I'm sorry. Maybe I shouldn't go with you. Please, I have to go back to my mom; she is crying."

He said, "We will take care of everything."

Again the feeling of peace came over me when He spoke. And it was so incredibly loving, safe, and powerful I just couldn't or didn't even want to leave this figure. Jesus was carrying me in His arms. The angel's wings surrounded us and they looked so soft and comfortable. But my mom's scream continued and became quickly faint as I was leaving. I felt like a big switch inside me flipped, like the main breaker switch you flip when the power goes out, and in that moment I decided I was definitely not going no matter how wonderful all of this felt. I looked at him again and said, "Please, please, just look at her."

He looked ahead.

I repeated and begged as loudly and as strongly as I could, "Please, please, you have to look at her; just look at her; she will never make it without me."

I also saw my grandpa Otto on his knees, holding his heart with one hand on the ground and the other hand over his chest. He was turned with his back to Hedy. She was alone, approximately a hundred feet away from him. My grandma Maya was standing to the right of Otto and had her hand on his back with her other hand covering her mouth. They were next to a large tree. As I watched, I did not see my dad, Walter, though I did see my brother sitting in the snow watching and then hanging his head down. From the hill where the booth was, there was a slope that went down and then flattened. Then another hill went down, and it flattened. Then again there is another hill. There was no way I could have seen what was happening where they were from standing on the top of the hill. Jesus and I were flying slightly above the hill and trees.

Easter 2014, It was springtime and I returned to see the hill. I walked from where we began to hold onto the tow rope to where it entered the tow rope booth. It was two thousand steps of my own, and walking at a pace in the spring with no snow, it took more than twenty minutes to get to the booth. Because of the deep accumulation of snow on that day of January 19 plus our exhaustion from hiking, I would safely estimate it took at least half and hour to reach the top of the hill from where they stood at the bottom of the hill. My parents and brother later told me it was a long time.

We flew higher but not very long. I arrived at this place that seemed like earth, but it was brighter and there was something different about it. It was absolutely natural and beautiful. I saw green grass and blue skies, with rolling hills in the distance. I saw a group of people wearing clothes that looked like robes, uniforms, or cloaks of some sort. They were wearing unique cloaks and they were grouped in a large circle. At first I thought it was about fifty people, but as we got closer, it was more like a hundred. They kept coming closer and closer and were chattering about my situation. They didn't walk; it was more of a high-speed glide. All were surprised I mentioned going back. They were kind and communicated with clear, thoughts, telepathic like. They could hear each other's hearts; they were all of one understanding, all on the same page. Communication for them was effortless, and all were understood perfectly. I noticed it's not like here on earth. On earth we spend so much time trying to communicate and be understood. We constantly correct, apologize and hope we have communicated completely, clearly and correctly. We have to back track, rethink what we expressed and hope it was understood the way we meant it. How many times does communication bring us together or tear us apart. Communication is everything. There in heaven it was effortless and clear. Perfect.

It looked similar to earth, but we were on the ground and could see for thirty miles.

I saw the most beautiful green grass, meadows, and rolling hills. When I arrived, the cloaked group, or council communicated with the three who brought me. Confused and ruffled about my response and persistence of wanting to go back, repeatedly asking each other and then me "Are you sure?" and saying, "This can't be happening"; "This is not allowed"; "Does anyone know what the rules are here?" "We'd better check with the others." There was uneasiness, yet they knew to ask.

We were never promised us we wouldn't suffer here on earth. We live in a world of light and darkness. But there is a divine place, I believe I saw and experienced some of it. The layers of distrust peeled away. It was amazing being there in the way I didn't have to look over my shoulder as a child as if someone was going to whisper to make fun of me or hurt or cheat me. It was great to see a place that let me know doing the right thing was honorable, not laughable, as it is here at times. No one will make fun of someone else in Heaven, not because of their looks; their lack of achievements; or their disabilities, mistakes, or shortcomings as we do here. In Heaven it is okay to achieve and be honorable and rewarded. Being in Heaven showed me that I don't have to ever worry about being attacked, dismissed, or disrespected by another. All relationships are had without selfish aspects. I can give all I want and no one will think I am stupid for it. I can do good things and not be laughed at. I can share, give, play, and be happy without apologizing or being accused of insincerity or having a hidden agenda. Telling the truth is accepted in Heaven; we don't have to hide parts of it or tell half of it. Heaven is a sincere, accepting, and honest place. Most of all, it is a loving place. The magnificent shining of Gods light, love and glory shined so bright it overshadowed everything. The light and love is so powerful and beautiful I will always remember it.

You see we spend so much time doing so many things, but in the end, we really are here to love one another and to understand what love is. In Heaven we learn the ways to help us become more loving. We also learn how we have misinterpreted the Bible, or how we have been misled, or used God's words incorrectly to damage one another. We learn the truth about God's love and ourselves.

Here we are more guarded, making it difficult to connect our hearts. We can learn from the beauty of the vulnerability of the heart. In Heaven it was beautiful to feel like a carefree child, to sing, to dance, to live without pain and suffering. Don't get me wrong; I do not want to go back or die. I love life and want to stay through thick and thin because life is an extraordinary gift to be cherished and grateful for. If we are unsure of our purpose, we can ask God to guide us. We need to keep our hearts and minds open when we wait for answers and trust. It is a practice, not to be done in one day, but each day, or as often as we can remember to do it. Spread love and joy. In Heaven I got to see how that works, and I can tell you it lights up the sky. The energy of love is like the most powerful fuel. There is always darkness close by, and it exists without effort and always seeks to put the light out, so it is important to try to make an effort to keep our lights on, if not for ourselves then for someone who may need us.

Over the hills another group of official-looking people came, with different-colored cloaks. The first group had soft gray cloaks, and the second group coming over the hill had white cloaks. Their walk was so fascinating like a kind of a high speed glide as they appeared from afar at a speed we cannot travel on earth. They just arrive when summoned.

The gray cloaks hoped for an answer. They had very specific abilities and were experts in what their duties were, and if it was out of their jurisdiction they summoned the next council of experts. It seemed each council had a purpose and boundaries of what they could or could not do. I knew that they heard my concerns and would do what was best. The white cloaks were informed after the grey cloaks. The white cloaks seemed sure of what to do and then became unsure. They asked each other, discussed as a group and then summoned more, and more, and more. He was still holding me. And the other two angels were like people, who had been at my side from the beginning. They were waiting for an answer. They were all very kind and compassionate, and exhibited the kind of love and faith that made me totally relax and trust completely.

I was amazed at how many white cloaks came. Then another group came, and soon it seemed as if they were coming in from different areas or towns. There were four or five the others looking for final decisions. They contemplated. They then approached Him, the two angels, and me and said, "You would go back for your mother and family?"

"Does she understand what this means for her?"

"The pain she may have to endure for the rest of her life?"

"We cannot promise she will not be crippled or ever have a life without excruciating pain."

"Does she understand how hard this would be for her?"

"Why, we rarely if ever see this behavior in a child, so what do we do with her?"

"She doesn't care about the pain; she is willing to take it. She is more worried about the pain of her mother and will sacrifice her life."

They said I was a sweetheart -- I heard the word "sweetheart" several times -- and then they looked time crunched again. The communication was like music without lyrics, speaking without words. It was like looking in someone's eyes and seeing their souls and understanding it completely. Then we both smile at one another with our eyes. There is no jealousy, no worries about being misunderstood. We never have our guards up because no one will ever hurt us. It feels so peaceful in the way we can say the most loving things to one another, believe them, and not worry if we've said too much or will scare others away. We can show as much love as we want. We are safe emotionally.

In this spiritual realm we don't worry about hidden agendas or competing with others. We can relax and totally be ourselves; our inner beauty is what we freely share. There is no need for pain or hurt. Time felt different, almost like it was non existent, and a funny thing that is was not the same as it is here.

When I returned, my mother really had to guard me because my heart was so innocently wide open and unprotected. I trusted that everyone was good. Heaven showed me what it is like to be able to open your heart completely and trust one another. I let my guard down. We don't have to research people on the Internet, try to figure out whether they are lying, and then feel we've been made a fool of later on. We don't hold grudges, we all wind up skipping and playing in the meadows together anyway so what's the point. Heaven is amazingly honest and you can be your true self.

On earth some are revered for being able to cleverly fool others or make money from cheating them. They're considered bright because they know how to rip off others. Heaven is the opposite of what is here. We can trust -- and we do. We don't have to worry that someone has ulterior or hidden, selfish motives. What a waste of time.

I learned that the Lord's Prayer tells us so much if we really listen and don't just memorize the words. Can we have it "On earth as it is in Heaven"? Can we create more balance here in these times? Can we create more honesty and trust with our free will? Yes we can because with God all things are possible. I have lived a miracle and was given so much love that I know exists for us all. I saw the power and glory and it is real and can do anything. Right now I would say we still all need good, healthy boundaries, which makes me sad after what I experienced. I had a bit of a hard time returning and learning how to be careful to love here. Carefully protecting myself from hurt has been an ongoing work of creating healthy boundaries. I have seen many times moments and situations of Heaven on Earth in people who have done beautiful genuine, unselfish acts of giving to others or sharing their kindness.

In Heaven love flows. There is music, laughter, and joy. The colors are like rainbows that illuminate. Our beings are beautiful in human form but our souls create our beauty, as our inner beauty becomes our outer beauty. It is what we see in each other and the ability to hold someone's hand without fear, to trust each other completely, to never have to doubt another's intentions. Truth, beauty, and all we hope and strive for exists, and we live together without any pain. It is not boring, but Heavenly. My heart felt so warm and full and I had no feelings of restlessness or uneasiness. Peace rules and gives the ability to enjoy living. Everyone in Heaven was working but not climbing a corporate ladder. The work was more like a mission to assist and support others. The work was humble and full of purpose for creating more light and healing. The forgiveness we learn in heaven is powerful.

There was definitely a need for work and a need for education, an enlightening education to bring us closer to one another, and to Him, so we can learn how to achieve true understanding, compassion, and forgiveness. Heaven let me know that loved ones are not ripped apart when we die. I understood we don't live our whole lives together loving each other, only to be torn apart in the end. Love is never ending and continues on far beyond our lives here. We are created by love. Of course there are people who abuse love using their free will to rape and murder, but this is not Gods doing, but of man alone.

Heaven showed me that we are not born alone, and do not die alone. We are born from a mother. There is no other way. I'm not sure how it works for everyone exactly when we die, but I am sure people are greeted with what is uniquely perfect and best for them. It is similar to childbirth. We are all born one way, not alone but through a mother. If you were to ask each mother about her child's delivery you will hear a unique story from each mother. But everyone has been born the same way attached to a woman and through a woman's body.

Heaven also showed me we don't have to live alone. There are billions of people on the planet, but even in our loneliest moments, we are loved completely by God. So we are never ever truly as alone as we think. No man is an island, and we are wired as humans to be together and love one another. Solitary confinement in prisons has been shown to cause mental illness. Human babies born perfectly healthy and given food and water will still fail to thrive if they are not held, cradled, and hugged. Studies show that isolation is very traumatic to humans, so God would not design our lives to be lived alone.

Faith is so beautiful when I see it in others. For me, it is not really faith anymore since I saw a piece of Heaven. It is technically more of a knowing. But those who have faith without ever seeing it are my heroes. They are so beautiful and strong. There is so much beautiful music and laughter in Heaven. It's not boring and sleepy. It is extraordinarily beautiful, powerful, uplifting, and rewarding.

So as I waited, they still did not want to make the decision and instead awaited a decision from God. During that time, I was shown around the landscape and learned more about Heaven. In the meantime, we waited. Finally they looked to the top one of that council for the final say, but he couldn't make the decision either. So they agreed to summon someone, and with great hesitance, like when you have to wake your dad from a nap, but you are afraid he will be really grumpy, so you contemplate whether it's worth it before you wake him up. "We have no choice; I will not, nor will anyone else make this decision. There is no law that will allow it." Then 4-5 went over the hills again and it got very quiet. The others just mingled with one another.

We waited, but I didn't know for what. I did, however, notice the smiles, the hugs, and the good fellowship amongst them all, nothing but kindness.

God communicated with me again, "Are you sure? This will be so hard for you. We can't promise you will be able to stay long, and we can tell you the pain will be overwhelming for you. We are so concerned for how hard this will be for you. Why would you do this to yourself?"

I answered, "It's for my mom; she won't make it without me. I don't care about the pain. Her pain will be greater than mine if I leave."

It was quiet, and I sure loved how I felt there. Who would ever want to leave? There are reasons people do not return after dying. Heaven showed me that God has a perfect system. I cannot know it all, but it all makes sense. There is so much more to our lives than we know. Sometimes we wonder why one dies and not another. Sometimes we are the answer to someone else's prayer and journey in life. God takes care of us all. When a child dies it is extremely hard, even though God is there with all the love He has. I like to think after all the goodness I saw that maybe there was a bigger purpose for that child. Maybe the child jumped into the world too soon and needed to return because Heaven needed that child more. I don't know but I'm sure whatever the reason, God is the Father and loves us all. I felt He would reunite us with our loved ones when it was the right time. To see that love is pure joy. Heaven showed me that God is part of everything: the leaves on the trees, the wind, the sunshine, the clouds, and the particles of life all around us. Our environment and nature hugs us with His love.

When we are disappointed, we must try to remember our big gift is free will, and He has to work to help us all despite our poor choices. He did not create all the things that are wrong and painful here on earth. We have free will and create our own famine, disease, and hate. He does not interfere unless we ask. So if we want help, we just need to ask. Help is always there, maybe not the way we think it is, but He will bring us help. We have weak moments of thought and loss of faith that can let evil or negativity grab a stronghold. Sometimes darkness grows stronger. Sometimes we find the way back to opening our hearts again. God's love always gives us a choice to come back and be forgiven and loved.

Then I heard a rumble in the sky and felt a wind. This large cloud-like mass of white light shot through and came toward us, and a large golden hand came through it. First it touched Jesus on the shoulder, and then touched my heart. "No promises can be made, but she will be permitted to try. Is that understood? You will return with great pain once you leave here. Is that understood?"

I replied with fullness in my heart, "Yes."

We flew back down quickly, and on the way He told me He would lay me back down. It would feel very cold, and I might feel a lot of pain, but I will be okay and He would stay with me until someone arrived.

CHAPTER 13

THE LIGHT

Here's how I can explain the beautiful divine light I experienced. They came to greet me with light around them. The light was blinding but pretty at first until I could adjust my eyes to it. It grew quickly and then drew me in to look deeper into it. The light had "life" in it, like an aura, and contained emotions, knowledge, and all that encompassed us, so we could gain understanding without words. As the "light being" shared Himself to allow us to recognize and completely understand Him, we also completely understand and recognize ourselves and are elated to be truly seen in all ways.

The light was bright, brilliant, and more beautiful and welcoming than any other light I had ever seen before or since. Now, when I see the clouds in the sky open up to yield rays of gold and white sunshine, I am reminded that Heaven is somewhat similar. It is as if the light tells me when someone good is coming toward me and I connect. The Being I will always know to be Jesus had extraordinary love that blended with the light and made it shine; love is the light. I began to feel, think, and recognize that our language is primitive in comparison to the communication in Heaven. Telepathy is probably as close as I can describe it here.

Jesus is so powerful in the way He made me feel and relax. It's as if every cell of my body, every need, every concern, every emotion, everything about me and my life is heard and understood in a matter of a moment. As the light shined brighter and got larger and closer to me, my understanding grew with it, and my protections and barriers peeled away. I was free to feel, see, and embrace Heaven's beauty without doubt or skepticism. The light surrounded and poured into me, and I poured into it as I realized I was part of this enormous light and it was now part of me. Today I still get tears of joy in my eyes when I think of Jesus and the light and love He came with. Its impact is so powerful it is hard to find the words, but luckily I have lived with this for so many years and I can say it has lasted all this time and grows stronger. The light is infused with a love and knowledge.

CHAPTER 14

MELCHIZEDEK AND HEAVEN'S LANDSCAPE

I also got to see another being of light in Heaven. He had a long white beard, a very chiseled face, a strong jaw and cheekbone definition, and unforgettable eyes. He was somewhat weathered looking, appeared older than Jesus, and had a serious demeanor, as if someone had just awakened him and it seemed he wasn't awakened often. He showed himself to me deliberately and purposefully during my stay. I knew he wanted me to focus on his physical features. When I turned away he would again make a point to show me his physical features close up. In fact, he gave me a memory of them so I would carry that memory with me after I returned. I did not at the time understand why but there is a purpose that will reveal itself exactly when it is suppose to. . His face was illuminated during our time together and faded when I was to see other things.

His old deep blue robe matched the deep blue sky. It was an indigo blue, a royal and regal looking color. He took me under my arms from behind, and glided me around off my feet and off his . I really don't know if he had feet I didn't look under his robe. I wondered if he was taking me to see any dead relatives, but I had no relatives who would have met me, and being an immigrant to the

United States, I had never met my great grandparents. I had one deceased grandfather, named Ernst, but I never met him before he died. So basically, I would not have known or recognized anyone in Heaven during that time. I guess instead I got to meet him. I don't know exactly why I got such a long experience with him.

When I returned from Heaven, I found his name to be Melchizedek. I spent time with him as he shared about his choice of appearing to me with old age and wisdom. He let me know there was some kind of hierarchy. He let me know that he was very wise and showed me he was in charge of training of some sort. It came to me that he showed age to correlate with wisdom and experience. I also understood the importance of knowledge. He had a special purpose that only belonged to him and what he is governed to do. He also had very specific purposes and gifts. There seemed to be a wind that blew back his white beard as we glided through the deep blue sky. The "wind" had no discomfort or chill, however; it just showed movement. I saw mostly Melchizedek's face, but soon saw an area that had buildings of some sort, which were understood to house enormous learning information. The materials there represented different levels and different stages of learning. It was the perfect education and maybe correctional system. It was a place of viewing past records to gain insights into truths and how to heal them. I believe they even house films of special experiences. The levels of learning takes place differently for everyone, as we are all having different experiences, yet the help is there to heal wounds and to enlighten and grow in spiritual love. Knowledge is powerful.

Melchizedek also showed me that place I call Heaven's landscape. I absorbed the beauty of the green rolling hills, lush trees, and the soft flowered meadows. I saw a special meadow with the colors of purple, yellow and white. It was a personally calming sight. Little did I know this meadow would be special for me later in my life? I realized it was winter when I left for Heaven. When I entered this new place with Jesus it was still sort of snowy colors, but slowly more colors entered and began to become more and more vibrant. It was similar to watching black and white television and then getting a color television. When I was a little girl I loved to hold a flower in my hand in my stroller and there were plenty of flowers all around the landscape of heaven to admire. I wanted to run and smell them all. I don't ever want to speak for God, but it seemed that the colors were introduced slowly as if to not want to frighten me of this new place. It seemed everything was perfectly done in such detail to make you feel safe and loved. The colors were similar as we see here on earth; they're just cleaner, brighter and more radiant in Heaven. The colors energy fills you with happiness. The colors and the appreciation for them and for nature filled me. The landscape brings peace and joy. While with Melchizedek I learned that nature is also an excellent teacher. It is one way we learn the rhythms and cycles of life. Nature holds many cures for healing ourselves. Nature holds many answers. I could strangely see the landscape for miles in Heaven, much like I can here when viewing the earth from a mountain, a building, or an airplane, except in Heaven I was on the ground.

Within Heaven's gorgeous landscape were different communities, or towns. I heard bells ring in the different towns. It appeared very much like here except more peaceful and more evolved. Everyone belonged and emitted a sense of feeling accepted. There are forms of work in Heaven. I realized the communities had a purpose and we can see those we knew who had passed over. They may not be in our communities, but when we communicate, they can appear, as can we.

The communities have rules and laws to protect us, even in Heaven. They have the most beautiful rolling hills, the sounds of the bells ringing, the gardens, the forests, and the fields of flowers. The communities did not appear crowded; crowds of people were not flying all over the place in chaos. Souls were not flying around lost. Instead there was organization, love, and peace. It was peaceful and full of beauty.

In addition, we do not have to worry that we can't find our loved ones or that they have forgotten us. We realize in heaven that things are done for a reason we do not always understand. We are able to understand if and when we are meant to. We can always ask and will get a response. No answer is still an answer, but if you question it, ask again and again. Listening is then important. The practice of learning to listen is important to receiving the answers.

Nearing the end of my stay in Heaven, I saw what I understood to be God's presence. I saw a white light, a radiant gold light around it, and when we heard from God, there was another gold light that was just a thick beam of light that looked like it was a golden hand actually over a mountain range. There is no mistaking God; and He is more tremendous than words can say.

Here on earth, we look for our life's purpose, but all we have to do is ask God for an answer when we feel stuck. Prayer is a powerful action and a way we communicate. We can ask for signs and guidance and for anything we need and the clarity and wisdom to see it. When God is in our lives, there is no disappointment. And of course free will reigns so we can choose to listen to His guidance or not. That's how much He loves us.

We also don't have to spend time analyzing why tragedies happen because we will find out all we need to know when we are supposed to know it. There is no need to carry a heavy burden, to feel persecuted, or to feel like God has been unjust to us. We are loved. Only good can come from a relationship with God.

I believe Melchizedek showed me he had much wisdom. I believe he shared some of them with me while spending time together and some have come to light over time. Little did I know the different telepathic communication during my time there would imprint on me throughout the rest of my life. Now, when I see something or hear something familiar, gut feelings, reactions misunderstood, words that appear when speaking, I know they all came from that the time I spent there, almost as if they had been downloaded into me. I have such a strong memory of the smells, touches, and feelings of pure love I had often searched for, especially during my youth. Melchizedek was unknown to me before this visit. I have since discovered more and more information unravels over my lifetime. Melchizedek was a teacher to me and I learned from him. I learned that communication is very often the cause when situations are problematic. Word injuries can happen when we are challenged communicating. Healing can also happen with word healing. It is our tool to connect in our life on earth, and how we express to one another. It can bring us together and solve so much, or it can destroy relationships in a moment. It requires both choice and wisdom. I learned we are all at different levels of spiritual awareness and different levels of learning and when we recognize this it often fosters more patience and forgiveness for one another. It was shared with me that everyone is offered ways to grow that are uniquely helpful to him or her. We repeat lessons when they are not learned. We are sometimes stripped down to nothing to see clearer and find the important things we need to help us on our journey. It was also shared that there is so much more help available than we can ever comprehend, and so many willing to help if we just ask.

CHAPTER 15

THE COUNCIL AND THE LAW

There are the laws of Heaven and the laws of man. In His arms, I saw a council, a hierarchy, and an order to things. People know and understand this order. They work; they have purpose and a function. There are experts in different divisions or different laws of the Heavenly system, and each person knows what he or she needs to do, and they operate within their own boundaries and carry out their own responsibilities. When they are unsure about what they are supposed to do, they ask questions to the group responsible for the laws.

The creator of this divine system was in an area far over the hills surrounded by a golden light and aura. The area was farther away than my eyes could see. I did not see where the angels lived or where anyone specifically lived for that matter. I wondered why the two angels I saw were men. I did not see the images of female angels we have in pictures here in my personal experience. I just knew there were communities because the people in the white cloaks came from different towns when they were summoned. I did see a family of people in a council who were there to help protect the children on earth. One was tall and slender, wore a long robe, and looked both serious and kind at the same time.

Different organizations served different purposes, both on earth and in Heaven, though some served only Heaven.

No information is ever lost in Heaven's council. There are records, and information is there for us to learn from. There was a strong sense of "Behave yourself and do the right thing to create more light." I was very mindful of not disrespecting God or His children, even though I knew I could ask forgiveness. I understood that it was very important to do good things as those nice deeds and nice people do matter. It is part of the work. While love feels amazing in Heaven, there is also a parental side of correcting wrongdoings, which is also done out of love. Earth is where parents are introduced to this concept, which is then carried through in Heaven. Here we learn how to love in a nurturing way and also in a tough way when it is needed for growth.

Ego is non-existent in the council of Heaven, and God, who judges us perfectly and in a loving manner, makes judgments. When I returned, I found I was no longer as judgmental a person; in fact I came back very understanding as a result of my visit. It feels out of place to judge others. It is much better to obtain more information to gain an understanding of a situation first. Ultimately all of us are given direction based on God's judgment of us, and I have found peace with that.

There was a very large tree in a forest in Heaven that looked like a warm shelter. The trunk is cut out of it and large enough for me to stand inside it. It somehow recognizes and attracts only those who are without compassion or conscience, those who have embraced darkness. These souls look to steal the hidden treasures in the tree when they think no one is watching. But when they enter, they are quickly sucked into the earth. It was like the tree was the first line of defense for sorting out dangerous beings.

When I walked inside it, nothing happened. But then I watched someone else go in get sucked down. Though I'm not sure what happens to these souls, I understand that God takes care of them, that there is a type of perfect justice. I can only report what I saw, but those who have been wronged on this earth will find a perfect justice in Heaven. Later in life I have read there is a tree of knowledge, and a tree of life and wondered if it was possible that it was one of those trees or a different one. I also learned that when there is confusion it is not from God. Confusion is a sign to ask for help to clear things up. I pray for clarity at times of questions, and for the ability to recognize the answer.

CHAPTER 16

RETURNING FROM HEAVENLY ARMS

When I returned, I discovered Jesus had laid me with my left cheek to the ground. It was cold and I had a terrible headache. I screamed as loud as I could. I could see the snow beneath me, turning red, and blood oozing so fast from my eyes that it covered them. I looked to Him and I wasn't afraid; He was right there. Soon the blood from my eyes oozed all around me, turning the snow red. I heard my mom's footsteps after what seemed to be a long time from the time I screamed. He left as my mom approached on His left side. He was facing me, and I thanked Him with all my heart. When I was with Jesus I did not miss my family. It sounds sad that I did not miss them, but it was more that Jesus filled me with so much love, and in heaven there was no sadness. I returned realizing that I was extremely grateful for life, but I could also definitely see why we don't want to return. When Hedy came to my side, she asked, "Susanne, who were you just talking to? I heard and someone else talking, who else was here? " I was covered in blood and smiled saying, " It was Jesus and angels, and they helped me " Hedy said "stop talking, and wow, how can it be you are you so peaceful and smiling?" I didn't have a chance to answer. "Never mind", Hedy said quickly, 'I think we should just keep quiet and rest now." It was the beginning of creating my secret by having to stuff down the experience and hold it in my heart.

I visited all kinds of places of worship looking to connect and find God's love I experienced. They said it was His house so as a child I figured He must be in there. I was on a quest to find the kind of love I missed from being in Heaven. It became often confusing to find that they had a business side and a vision and perception a single man or team had created. Somehow when money became the focus I was sad. So I had to accept I might never find it here. Plus, money was always involved. There is no money in Heaven. I longed to find that kind of connection I had in Heaven here on earth. I used to be overwhelmingly lonely in my experience. After all, who here could truly relate to me? How could I expect understanding from something so uncommon? I hadn't heard of anyone dying and returning from Heaven. It definitely wasn't discussed when I was growing up. As a child, at first returning I thought everyone knew what I knew and saw it too, but I learned in time that was not the case.

To this day, I am still full of the light Heaven shone on me. Later on, as a child I was exposed to a prayer called the Lords prayer as it was so commonly used so I listened to it. It really does tell us things can be done on earth as they are in Heaven. It can begin within our own families, friends, and strangers we personally meet. People have asked me many times how I knew their feelings. It is so important to see the pain of others and make them feel connected. Patients have looked into my eyes and said to me in their last days, "I feel at ease now that you are here." One of my patients was a Catholic priest with terminal cancer, who said to me, "I can rest now; you make me feel safe." Others have told me the same thing. I returned with heightened senses. It's hard to describe but the senses are heightened with purpose. It changed me to be very sensitive for living things. It brought and awareness that understands , an ability to listen to the light and allow it to light my path and others. Beyond the words spoken by another, I became able to see and feel an issue with amazing and keen insight. Returning I began to notice I was able to connect and feel my relationship strongly. I was able to relax and trust love. I realized loving work matters. Learning how to love and be loved is important. Others who never knew this story or secret remind me of my differences. I learned my differences and gifts over time. I still do. They are still respectfully private to me. They grow and are absolutely amazing and beautiful. At this time I have to share what I feel is important in this story and the focus is love and inspiring or awakening your hearts and gifts.

My family and others have also seen a change in me. They see me as someone who listens closely. When people have asked my advice, they all say that I can see their core, what's really going on in their hearts, what's really causing their problems, when even they don't know. "Ask Sue; she will help you." My life has been changed forever. I can also say I returned with extraordinary gifts from the light that I could not put words to, yet. I felt I had been included into a spiritual realm and given special awareness and enlightenment.

The messages I received are woven within this story, but one special message I personally received was

> "LOVINGLY SHARE THIS WITH OTHERS"
> "ANYONES LIFE YOU TOUCH WILL ONLY BENEFIT FROM IT.".

This is some of my work I was sent back to do. To inspire people to bring forth their gifts and let their light shine. To lead them to where there is pure light and love whenever they need or want it.

To tell how it will work through you, for you, and within you. We all have meaningful work and we can choose to do it. By shining my light I hope to inspire others to do the same. Realizing life can be tough at times my gift is to help by sharing this experience. I believe there are amazing gifts inside each and every one. There are signs of this in many ways, and even in the Bible. 1 Timothy 4:14 "Neglect not the gifts inside thee." So my mission is to bring hope and to inspire and remind people of their gifts, and love. You are special, loved and your life matters!

CHAPTER 17

THE HOSPITAL

I could hear my mom calling for help. "She is alive! Hurry! Please hurry!" They all came right behind her, and with blankets.

"Don't move or touch her!" Hedy said. "Be very careful."

My dad picked me up with the help of a young man named Steve. He was the volunteer security guard in the community. He had a car with a light he could put on to top of it. He apologized for taking so long; he had to shovel the snow out of his driveway. He put my mom and me in the backseat. I was lying with my head across the seat, and she squeezed in next to me. "Watch her neck. Don't move her too much. Drive as fast as you can." I was so happy to feel my mom's hand near me. She was trying to hum and talk like nothing happened, telling me everything will be all right.

Later Hedy told me that for a long time, it was silent after I went up the hill because everyone thought I was dead. Hedy said she wanted to come up right away but Maya grabbed her, held her tight, and told her sternly that she was not going up the hill to see a dead child. "No mother should see their little girl dead," Maya said. Later Maya told something or us that she wanted to spare Hedy in case I had been decapitated. She was just protecting Hedy from what they felt would have been a gruesome sight.

She told Steve to drive fast but be careful. On the road, his light was causing others on the highway to slow down because everyone thought he was a real cop and they were afraid of getting a speeding ticket. "Sigh," he said. "This always happens when I leave the club."

My mom grew very tense but disguised it from me. She continued to put her hand on my face to compress the blood that was pouring out. I asked about my dog Heidi. My mom didn't know where she was but told me not to worry. "This is ridiculous," she said. "How long is it going to take to get there?"

"The nearest hospital is in New York," Steve said.

"Figures," said my mom.

I was in a lot of pain, but had so much love in my heart for my mom and family.

We arrived at the Emergency Room. A big team of people came out with a stretcher to correctly lift me. I made it. There were so many people around me -- nuns too -- all saying what a miracle it was that I was alive.

I had a better understanding of all the procedures they did after I became a registered nurse. I remember the hospital staff wearing scrubs, hats, and masks; performing a scan; and getting the operating room ready. My mom's stretcher was right next to mine. They said she was so hysterical she collapsed and they had to give her something to help her sleep. As for me, I was just hoping to make it home in time to see the Mod Squad television show I routinely watched with my grandma.

They checked my brain functions and asked lots of questions. I watched them cut off my shirt to put a gown on then wring and me my shirt out in the sink. The yellow mock turtleneck I was wearing was bright red because it was covered in so much blood. The nurse saw me looking and turned her face of horror into a smile and comforted me. Everyone was in a rush and many people kept coming to see me.

Finally I was rushed to the operating room, and the team of doctors around me was all talking about the swelling on my temples. There were two large circular protrusions about four centimeters, covering the entire temple area on each side of my head. They performed some brain function tests and said if the swelling did not go down in twenty-four hours, I would die. They were kind to me as they worked in large groups very fast, but expected my condition to decline rapidly. They talked about a brain bleed, paralysis, and yet the tests proved nothing.

They put forty-four stitches over my eye, and my neck had no skin on it. One side of my body was paralyzed. The other side was weak but sort of okay, but I still couldn't move. I was breathing fine, though.

While my mom was still drowsy, she got off her stretcher, and came to see me. I honestly don't remember much after that. The last thing I said before going into the operating room was, "Where is Heidi?" My mom said she did not know, and I said, "Make sure you find her."

After all was done, lots of people were coming to see me because I had miraculously recovered, and no one could explain why. The nuns came and prayed over me, and were so excited to meet me. Everyone had such a joy for me, as if they were seeing their own miracle. Love, hope, and faith exploded inside their doubting minds. The surgeons and doctors said, "Put a plaque up in this hospital, in her name; she is a living medical miracle case." This all happened in St. Francis hospital in New York. Later the name would be changed to Bon Secure.

My dad phoned the hospital to say he found Heidi lying in the blueberry bushes, and he thanked me for reminding him of her or she would have frozen to death. He said I saved Heidi's life.

Otto said he fell to his knees with chest pains, and soon after saw my scarf fly down the hill like a flag, perfectly straight, perfectly untangled. He spent a lot of time and intense focus trying to figure out the logical mechanics, the logical explanation, of how I could be alive, as he was one of the best mechanical engineers around (I'm told he made a car for the Queen of England and brought it to her personally). He was not a spiritual or a religious man, so he checked the booth and the machinery. He said my survival was impossible, and if he hadn't seen it himself, he would have never believed it. It was for him a miracle that his and Maya's granddaughter lived, and Hedy and Walter's girl lived.

I felt illuminated and full of love. That miracle imprinted itself on all of us in different ways, but the one thing we all shared was that we all believed in miracles.

No one in my family wanted to hear me talk about it, though. They thought it would upset me too much. So they kept me quiet and rested. When I did try to talk about it, however, their eyes twinkled and then dimmed. So for the most part, I was alone with the euphoria of comfort I could not share from my experience in Heaven. They just couldn't listen to it. Their eyes would fill with tears if they only listened for a second.

As I tried to convince my mother of all the amazing news I had, she said, " I need you to stop talking about this, I know it was real, but you need to promise not to tell anyone. It will not be good for you to be asked about it and relive this deadly accident over and over again. It was too horrible and too much trauma. Please let's just take the miracle and celebrate privately. We need to move past this and never look back. We need to forget about the accident and what you experienced. You can keep it in your heart. But promise me you will never tell anyone, I don't know, maybe when you are older. Trust me." I knew now that I had to keep this bigger than life spiritual journey a secret, and lock it away. I trusted my mother and honored her wishes. My memory could not be erased. The experience grew and the love and light made me stronger.

CHAPTER 18

THE PARALYSIS AT HOME

When I arrived home I was placed on the couch in the family room, though my family was afraid of moving me too much. I was stared at, whispered about, and my family was ridden with the unknown of what would or could happen. To this day, the mention of this ski accident is the only time I have seen my family's eyes well up with tears. Forty years later it still brings a look of horror and tears to their eyes within a second and the conversation never gets past the first line. It freezes them like a freeze frame in a film.

I had more than forty stitches in my right eyebrow. The right side of my head was strangely and completely numb for months. I joked over and over that someone could pull my hair, or for that matter, stick a knife in my head and I wouldn't feel it. My eyebrow had a scar that I now call my Harry Potter scar.

I remember how love saved and protected me. I was unable to walk, so I had to call for assistance if I had to go to the bathroom. That was actually the highlight of my day. I could use my arms but I was unable to write, but my homework was sent home from school. They term paralysis was used. I had very limited motor skills. My friend and neighbor Linda would deliver it sometimes. Linda who

I walked to school with everyday came to visit and would initially sit by the couch I laid on and a blanket covered my legs. . One day, however, Linda wept on my legs. I would laugh it off, and try my best to make her laugh, but I couldn't. I couldn't make anyone feel better about what happened to me. People would just stare, smile with tear-filled eyes, and run to another room. Linda's visits brought me comfort and a life line to my days before the accident.

I'm told I had severe headaches and suffered severe pain, but I do not remember the pain. That period of my recovery was a big blur to me. I was still euphoric about all the love and light I experienced and returning back to life. There was no way I was going to complain about anything. I was so grateful I felt so lucky.

CHAPTER 19

ANOTHER MIRACLE AND MIRACLES ALL AROUND

In time, I was moved to my bedroom. I spent a lot of time alone, but people frequently checked on me. One day my mom had left the house briefly, and when she came home, I was sitting up on the couch. She looked as if she'd just seen a ghost and her face turned pale. "How did you sit up like that?" she asked.

"Oh I forgot," I answered. "I must have just not laid back down after going to the bathroom."

She said, "You walked to the bathroom by yourself?"

"Yes," I replied. As I answered, I realized what had happened.

She put both hands on top of her head and shouted, "I don't believe it!" She kept saying this to herself over and over. "Susanne, please, please never do that again."

I said, "Don't worry; I will show you I can."

She ran to stop me from getting up, but I got up and walked to the bathroom as if I had never been in that accident. I went to the kitchen and walked all around the house, laughing. Hedy half believed it was a miracle, but half of her wanted to tell me to lie back down. As she watched me, however, she almost fainted with delight, chanting, "This is an absolute miracle. I can't believe I'm seeing this." The rest of my family witnessed it, too, and we all began cheering about the miracle.

All the pain and any limits to my mobility disappeared overnight. As a matter of fact, I went on to pursue gymnastics and swim team again that summer. I was asked to rest, but all I wanted to do was run. No one could believe the overnight change. It was like waking from a coma and going outside to play tennis.

We went to the house in the Poconos that summer, and excitedly I was able to walk outside. Those in the Poconos had seen me the summer before this happened. When they saw me again, they were almost disappointed. "I heard she was paralyzed," people would say, "all banged up and disfigured." Well to see me that summer they would have never known, except I had to be careful of my neck and head. I still had some numbness in the right side, and my scar well....

There are miracles all around. I now take time to look for them, and passionately say I am grateful for them. Sometimes when I am almost in a terrible car accident or in a car accident and I or those I love survive, that is a miracle. Life can change on a dime, and all the times I have said 'Wow, that was lucky" those are the miracles. Those times when things could have gone terribly but do not, those are the miracles. I practice gratitude for many of those moments, and feel the great love from above embrace me. Miracles are everywhere, everyday and it is so sad that sometimes we have to loose something wonderful to recognize the miracle we had.

CHAPTER 20

THE MEAN RECEPTION, AND THE BLESSING OF A MOM

I was walking by the lake, celebrating just being alive, like I do every moment of every day. So many beautiful people, friends, relatives, neighbors came to see me. They brought me gifts and gave me hugs and smiles and genuine comfort with their compassion and kindness. What I didn't expect was what happened when I ran into some pre-teen girls, who I knew and thought they would be happy to see me. Well, I was shocked at their reaction.

One girl said, "Oh you look fine" in a jealous Snow White's stepmother kind of tone. "I thought you would look a lot worse, little miss beauty queen." When I shared the happiness of my recovery, I anticipated their faces would be beaming with joy, but the Snow White's stepmother look only got worse. So I revealed more to them, thinking they would be happy for me at some point. Nope, there was an awkward silence when I was finished, and then she spoke. "Did you know we made up a song about you while you were injured this winter?"

I was still hoping for some shared wonderful embrace, so excitedly, and without an ounce of caution, I thought it would be compassionate. She said, "Oh yes we did," and smiled.

I smiled back, thinking things may turn around for the best.

She said, "Yes and we all made it up together. We each helped in making many verses of this song and we sang it about you all winter."

I thought then that I misread the ugly stepmother stares. And with a joyful heart, I was so excited to be loved and accepted by my peers. "Wow," I said, "that is so nice. I can't believe you did that."

"Yes, we will sing it for you," she said with a smile. "Ready girls?"

They all smiled, all five, and when I said, "Sure, I would love to hear it," they began....

It went to the tune of "Jesus Christ Super Star."

Jesus Christ super star,

(Loudly accentuated) who the HELL do you think you are?

Jesus Christ, super star, walks with a wiggle and she needs a bra.
Jesus Christ super star,
We sure wish you'd been hit by a car.

Well you get the point. There were many more verses, but somewhere in there I went numb and couldn't breathe. I was thinking of how protected and loved I was all the time before this, the fresh memory of Heaven's love still in every cell of my body. Now I had been struck down to remember I was definitely not in Heaven anymore. I struggled missing Heaven in that moment, just as we all do when another chooses to put us down.

I walked home up the mountain, completely alone, feeling as if I was spinning, dizzy, as if the wind had been knocked out of me. I felt very unsteady on my feet. But I just kept walking. Step after step I knew I'd reach the front door of my house, and I could safely collapse in my mother's arms. I don't know what I would have done if I didn't have her. I have such sympathy for children without mothers, or good mothers, and I appreciate having one so much. Good mothers do the work of angels in Heaven. Being held by her feels like being held by an angel.

I was devastated for a while, and the world lost a lot of color that day. It became gray. The negativity was so mean. After my mom spoke with me, and I decided to stay home for a few days, I became strong again. She relit my light with compassion, hugs, and a listening ear. With help from my experience in Heaven, I remembered that their behavior is a reflection of them, not of me. I would not let their weakness deter my new-found strength, and continued to be strong. I continued to believe in kindness and love, and in appreciation of the gift of a second chance at life, to go for everything I wanted. After the short-term shock, I forgave them in my heart, and saw the powerlessness of them.

I realized the importance of Heaven on earth, the moments of a mom's hug, the moments when a family member or friend gives us a kind word when we are down. Add faith to that, and remain true to not becoming like those who ridicule you, and you have a recipe for success. Don't go into their hamster wheel and get ugly like they are. Stay beautiful, as you were meant to be loved and cherished. If others don't love you, it is a reflection on them, not on you. There's a lot of ugly projection in the world. If you listen, people will tell you who they are.

In Heaven there are no cliques, no groups of exclusion, or secretive groups, like so many girls and ladies have here on earth. Heaven doesn't make people feel excluded, overlooked, forgotten, or invisible. Why do people exclude others or have groups where not everyone is welcome? I appreciate groups that are open so all those with common interests can join.

CHAPTER 21

FINDING PEACE IN BEING ALONE

I spent the summer to myself, walking with gratitude for every bird that sang. Don't get me wrong; people's harsh words hurt sometimes, and no one is immune to them, but that's why we need good people and God's love around us. I can choose to be happy just as easily as I can choose to be miserable. While I try to teach this choice to those who choose to be miserable, if they persist in wallowing in their misery, unfortunately, as much as they need the love of God, I can't make the choice for them, and at that point, I need to avoid them. It's important to learn that boundary.

This is why I did not socialize with my former group of friends from swim team that summer, and I left them to wonder why. I was fine by myself -- happy, content, and peaceful. I learned to like being alone and quiet, making joy in myself and with myself. I did come upon a full-figured, older girl named Francine. She was sixteen, which was "old" to an eleven-year-old. I told her I was almost twelve, though, hoping she would be my friend. She was very shy, but we gradually became friends. She had big beautiful hips, and a smaller bust, long straight blond-brown hair that lay over her shoulders, and a deep voice. People made her to feel ugly, too, because they couldn't see how beautiful she was inside. Every day, I told Francine something I saw in her that was "pretty."

She secretly like a boy named Danny, but said he would never go for an "ugly" girl. I just kept telling her she was beautiful, and making her laugh. By the second to last week of the summer, Francine started wearing a little makeup and doing her hair, and her own beautiful smile emerged. Her inner confidence was growing. She even started bragging a little about her talents and walking with a swag. She had begun loving herself, and Danny took notice. He told her he liked the way she smiled and he liked her sense of humor. Danny asked her out, and the two of them dated that summer, maybe longer for all I know. With kind words and acceptance, Francine had bloomed. She is beautiful; everyone who is kind and compassionate is.

A real friend makes you feel beautiful until you begin to see it in yourself. A real friend is not competitive with you, and will relight your light if it goes out. Since Angeline, I have made more and more friends who have been isolated by bullies – the pain of their hurtful remarks, their putdowns. They have no idea how much they hurt others. They might as well shoot people with a stun gun; it would hurt less.

My new friends and I enjoyed a safe and quiet summer together, just being ourselves with no one to impress. We played backgammon on the beach and enjoyed each other's personality; looks didn't matter one bit. It was the best summer I ever had because I made the nicest of friends. At first, they didn't trust me as I was the beauty queen of the town, but soon they did, and my inner beauty was finally seen. Seeing someone's inner beauty more than their outer beauty matters more to me than anything else. That's what I look for in relationships.

We left that summer and my transformation continued. I now wanted real friends, ones who were there for one another when we were down. I felt in my heart those were the only friends worth having. I learned the difference between givers and users, friends who used me to get to know some boy or drop my name if it served them. Nonetheless, I continued searching for true friends, without letting the disappointments stop me.

Since my beauty queen days, I have become uneasy with those who need to make a constant showing of physical perfection and win awards for beauty. Even at my young age then, I began to see my grandfather's point of view. I still had a lot to learn, but what a wise beautiful man. I valued his perspective deeper and more.

I also learned the power of prayer. They really are heard. We can use prayer all day, every day. We pray and speak honest and openly just like we would to a friend. We don't need to add a formal tone to our prayers, we don't need to be afraid how we sound, and we don't need to be afraid to pray wherever we are. But please remember not to get angry if you don't get everything you want right away. We need to trust.

I also found the beginning of seventh grade was the perfect teenage time to pray, as I faced another challenge being stressed out by the meanness of teens. Parents can be so helpful by being available for those teen-year talks because all teens are self-conscious, whether they are "popular" or not. One boy in my math class called me Frankenstein, day in and day out, but remember, I'd reached the point of believing beauty was superficial. He knew my looks were due to an accident. Thanks to Opa, I survived just fine by focusing on other things, the good things.

I laid low and blended in quietly in junior high. "Accomplishment" took on a whole new meaning. I only took credit for accomplishing something through some kind of effort, not through my looks. I shocked my family, including my poor mother, particularly when I insisted on taking gymnastics again. She bit her lip on the issue, as she probably thought I would never be able to compete in gymnastics again, but that didn't stop me. I practiced and practiced in my back yard, and in my basement on that old gym mat I had, while Hedy just stuffed away her personal fears and allowed me to try. No doubt she had every reason to be afraid, but she unselfishly kept her reasons to herself. I began playing the piano again and singing in the chorus. It all seemed richer to me than it was before my accident. God had given me a second chance at life, and I was grateful to be alive. Even though the pains and frustrations also felt deeper, my sensitivity toward others had become stronger, and my joys much sweeter. Even though at times I got frustrated when people were mean to each other, and wondered why earth couldn't be more like Heaven, my appreciation of life will never disappear.

After the accident, "Why not me?" became part of my vocabulary rather than "Poor me" or "Why me?" When I saw people accomplish things that inspired me, or things that looked fun and interesting, instead of saying, "Oh I can't do that; I don't know how," I continued to say, "Why can't I do that? Are good things just for others? Are those people better, more deserving, or more worthy than I am?"

With this new attitude, if I wanted to try something new, I did, and I didn't give up easily. That's how I learned the next lesson, that none of us are good at everything. But I tried. Thanks to my accident, I was spared of being the girl who just sat back and watched. I knew time mattered. Insecurities are fleeting, so I didn't get entangled in them for long. I knew confidence was all in my mind. Everything is not just for other people because I'm worthy, as well.

I prayed before I did some things. Instead of looking to others for answers, and receiving opinions based on their experiences. One year, I tried out for cheerleading. One hundred and fifty girls tried out, and there were only twelve spots, and only six of those were available to my class because the older girls were guaranteed their spots. Time passes so quickly, and I knew I may never get another chance to try cheerleading, so I seized the day. Besides, I had such passion for gymnastics and cheerleading seemed to be the only gymnastics-related sport available to girls. So I was going to try out when the time came.

I knew the heavenly love would always love me and help me, so it was good to try my best. If something didn't go my way, then I did all I could and it probably wasn't meant to be. That minimizes our own regrets and gives us a chance to see another door open.

The key is faith. It is loving and believing even when everything is not going the way we think it should. I look deeper for the good and trust that it is there. God is helping us; we are just not conscious enough to see it, perhaps due to our own negative patterns and thoughts. Faith is not giving up in difficult times. All of us can choose the easy road of getting angry and blaming God. There are bullies throughout life, and they hurt. But by not becoming one of them, you are amazing and beautiful, and by getting up in the morning and surviving them, you are a hero. You have a big blanket of love that is all around you.

CHAPTER 22

THE SEARCH FOR HEAVEN ON EARTH (FEELING THE LOSS) SEARCHING FOR PLACES OF WORSHIP

I continued to search for Heaven on earth. I would sneak out on Sunday mornings and check out all the different kind of churches because I believed love in people must still exist, and it had to be in those church buildings.

Sometimes I felt so lonely and disappointed on Sunday mornings. I did enjoy the spirit of love, people saying, "peace be with you" and giving a handshake, but I missed the feeling of being completely understood in Heaven, without words. Here we always have to explain what we really mean. We pick people and their words apart, and we can't know one another's true intentions even when we look in their eyes and feel it in our hearts. No one even has to speak in Heaven; everything comes from our hearts. Here we're called "naive" and "stupid" for trusting what we see and feel. The master manipulators are the ones who are praised for preying on the open and innocent. But in Heaven, I saw radiant smiles without a hint of jealousy or "what's in it for me?" Here I see a constant lack of gratitude and a sense of entitlement, as if people get where they are without any help from God or anyone else. People are so busy grabbing for money that they don't see others' needs, something that is totally absent in Heaven. Instead they get hung up on words or inappropriate expressions, or their inability to express anything at all.

I asked my parents to join me at church. They were usually chewing bagels and cream cheese or a danish on Sunday mornings and wanted to have a day to catch up on laundry. My dad said religion has been at the root of some of the most horrific wars. He also said people should just live a good life by their actions, and by example; they are their own temple. Mom was turned off by religion because she said everyone always wants money. She said the more she gave, the more they asked and then used God's name to guilt her. She said churches were full of so many phony people trying to confess what they've done wrong. "All they have to do is say they're sorry," she said. "It just gives them the right to do bad things. What about thinking before you act or speak? My own home can be my church, and I can pray anywhere I like. God is everywhere."

Okay, so they are not going. But I had to go; I felt driven to go. So I asked my parents what religion we were. My Mom said her side of the family was strict Catholic. An uncle or a cousin was somebody in the Vatican, and she remembered the "smoke" waved over people during the services. She remembered lots of money, jewels, and decorations. She said it seemed too fancy. Dad said we were Protestant, plain and simple, but no one ever went to church. The war and survival made it pretty impossible when they were growing up. The topic of church was usually cut short. They spoke and stopped and the door closed.

But I had seen Heaven. I was in Jesus' arms. I had seen angels and the councils. I yearned to be amongst them and spiritual people. So I asked my parents if they minded if I go to any of the churches nearby by myself. My dad always had a sense of wit and humor, and said with a pat on the back and a gentle voice, "No, go ahead, sweetheart. You will be our family representative." So on I marched by myself on Sunday mornings.

I went to a church that looked pretty on the outside. It was white with two big, red double doors. I always had a thing for a red door, and my dad was inspired by my passion so he painted the inside of our door red. I kept wondering if I could find the religion my family and I needed. I was open to them all. I knew if I searched long and hard enough, the right one would come through and it would feel like that day on the ski hill.

The Baptist church was happy. It had lots of people and a fun Sunday school. We had ice cream socials on Friday nights in different people's homes. I would walk or get a ride from a classmate. We had all kinds of ice cream and toppings and made our own sundaes. It was Heaven (ha). Well, it tasted good anyway; especially considering my mom was a health nut so we didn't eat junk food, not after Robert had been diagnosed with hyperglycemia.

Each classroom had a piano. I liked the music, and the people were warm and friendly. *Maybe this could be it,* I thought. They seemed to focus on a lot of socializing and family, but the teachings were rushed, and we were always doing plays and activities to raise money. Nonetheless, I felt at home; I felt the teachings were beautiful when they were given. *Wow, they are talking about Heaven and God!* I thought.

One night I went to an ice cream social at someone's beautiful home, and came to church the next day. We had been preparing for baptism. Funny but I still did not really understand what that meant. When I asked, the teacher said, "Honey, we have been preparing for this all along. The ceremony of baptism is in eight weeks. Where are your parents? What is your name again? Come to think of it, I don't think I've ever seen you here with your parents."

I had been attending regularly for months and months, so I did not understand why the teacher did not know my name. I said, "My parents do not attend, but I do every week."

The teacher responded, "Honey, have you been given offering packages?"

I said, "No, but I put money in the dish.

The teacher asked, "Have you ever been baptized?"

I said, "Yes, as a baby, for protection my mom said."

Then the teacher said, "Sweetheart, you need to leave. I'm sorry; you are not welcome in this church. Just go home, okay? And don't come back."

I cried, wiping my tears on the way home, thinking and talking to myself. *People can get thrown out of church? I will miss the ice cream sundae parties.*

It was an impression I will never forget. I realized the teacher wanted my parents there, but I was wondering what that meant.

Since I had to walk to church every Sunday, I could only go to "churches" within walking distance. I went to a Jewish Synagogue, with all the hugging, but had to sit in the back with the women, and they wanted my parents, too. Then I went to a Catholic church…or two with big stained glass windows, robes and history.

I went to every place of worship I could find within walking distance and lived in a bedroom commuter town outside New York City, so I had several places of worship to choose from. I was lucky to have visited a dozen. But I could not stay in God's home without making more monetary contributions, not as a youth, and not without my parents. So I went to a Moravian church down the street, near my elementary school. I didn't know what all the different names were. I didn't know the difference between Catholic, Moravian, Lutheran, Baptist, Episcopalian, Presbyterian, Temple, etc., and I was getting more and more confused. Was I supposed to go to a particular church just because I was born into it? Was I allowed to go to any place of worship? What's the difference? What did they all mean? Why are they separate and different names? Well I guess we all sit at different lunch tables in school depending where we are most comfortable, but we all eat lunch. It was really hard getting kicked out of God's house, but I kept trying. So, the Moravian church welcomed me and didn't have a problem with my parents not coming. My parents called them and said it was okay for me to attend there, so this church let me stay. The pastor was new.

I went to confirmation classes there. It was something I had to do at age fourteen. My parents said it was now my choice to say I have Jesus in my heart, and to do this. Of course he was in my heart so I did it. All this structure, I didn't know what it all meant. Plus I felt stupid when they looked at me funny for not knowing or not being aware of their system. *So is this God's house?* I wondered. *Is this a business? Both? Is it the pastor's house? Whose version or interpretation of God's word is this?* No matter which church I attended, however, people treated me nicer if I came more often. If I missed, people looked at me like "where were you?" It didn't feel bad; it just was not what I hoped for. We spent maybe forty-five minutes a week together. The rest was I don't know what. And once people stepped outside the church, they acted like they didn't know each other that well. Different boundaries. Not much passion at times. Some people acted like they were closer to God than others because they showed up more, or paid more money.

> The religions and the people I had seen at a young age had the undercurrent of love, devotion and commitment. They had different rules and laws. They had different structures to house their different beliefs, and different rules for showing dedication and commitment. Some people's hearts were tired and closed and they just "went through the motions." Others were full of joy and couldn't do enough.

I saw that different preachers could interpret scripture beautifully, though sometimes differently. So the source of the information and the condition of the person's heart and mind are crucial. My gut often tells me when something isn't right, and if I'm in doubt, I ask God. He always gives me a nudge. Pay attention to the warning bells He gives you: the discomfort, the uneasiness, the nausea, the headaches, the stiff necks, the restlessness, and the anxiety. They are telling you to look deeper and not just take what is served you as truth. Be sure you are well enough to receive information properly and they are well enough to deliver it. Be around people who want to be positive and uplifting.

God, His angels, His master angels, and the universe – is always there to assist you They can't help but intervene and never get tired of it, if you ask. We are given free will and the choice to choose, so they are willing to wait until we ask.

The bottom line is that I realized at a young age the earth was a battlefield of light and dark. I learned that sometimes we stop trusting and stop connecting when we are hurt. We stop being open and vulnerable. But the negative wins if we don't return to being vulnerable and open to love again. If we build too many boundaries, darkness will work to shut us down and that is another reason we should love one another. In those times we can assist each other to keep our light on.

Anyway in my generation we had Sunday school. The teacher dedicated his time to teaching Sunday school. He had the challenge of reaching us teenagers; all of us were awkward, cynical, aloof, and self-absorbed. I finished confirmation classes and was prepared to confirm my faith in a ceremony that would make me able to say out loud what I believe, finally. I was old enough to choose whether to attend. My parents, who I actually never heard them say the name Jesus, were no longer my spiritual teachers. I was ready to take responsibility for my beliefs and as a child in those days it was done officially according to the church.

We went on a weekend retreat as a group, in a nice setting, a building in an upscale area. I was afraid to tell or ask too much. Once when we gathered in our group for prayer, in a large circle, a girl began to speak and pray in a weird language. They called it tongues. She had no memory of speaking that way when prayer ended. During the prayer, I quietly felt Jesus' hand on my left shoulder. I felt so happy I cried. It reassured me that I still was connected to it all. I felt humble, greatly honored, and comforted. It was like it was in Heaven. *It's not far away; He's not far away.*

The week before confirmation, however, my pastor sent me a letter saying I was not going to be confirmed. He felt I did not take it seriously enough, and that I was too quiet. He stated I had to be more forthcoming and felt I was more interested in outside things. I knew what he was saying because he made many remarks about me being "pretty" and "cute." So to him I was a superficial airhead. I sat down with my mom and she encouraged me to write a letter back because I felt falsely judged.

In my own words, I asked Jesus for help in writing the letter. He led me to share a very small portion of the skiing accident and my life-after-death experience. I was told it was powerful. The pastor said he went into seclusion and prayed over it for almost two weeks, awaiting an answer from God. Then he phoned me and invited me to his house. He stared at me for a while and thanked me for having him go into such deep prayer over this decision. He said a verse came to him while he was in prayer for me, and he gave it to me as my confirmation verse. He opened up to me and told me he was a former gang-like person, who carried a chain and beat people when they couldn't pay back money they had borrowed. He found God and his wife and became a missionary. He apologized profusely.

I was confirmed with the class. Sometimes I got turned off by the people in the church, sometimes I loved it, but I managed not to let the balancing act of good and bad destroy my love or deter me in my spiritual journey and worship, even when some people were less than kind.

I learned so much my fourteenth year on this earth. Now confirmed by an earthly spiritual house called church, even though I already made my confirmation long before when I was in heaven. I went to junior high school, made the cheerleading squad, and did not retaliate when that boy called me Frankenstein. He actually asked me out on a date, though I politely declined.

I think during my search for Heaven on Earth I found love can be found everywhere and it was what shined through in many ways in different places and people. It was the love that was expressed and shared that was the most beautiful reminder and closest to heaven. It was in the miracles and beauty of nature. Everything about my life and spirituality changed to a level that I did not know where exactly I fit in here with other people sometimes, but I know I have my relationship first hand.

CHAPTER 23

HOW TO PICK A CAREER IN HIGH SCHOOL

Of course, the big question upon graduating high school is "What do you want to be for the rest of your life?" The school guidance counselor always seemed busy and would direct me to pick up some pamphlets off the coffee table in the hallway, so I really never spent much time with him. There was also a rumor that he made advances toward a student, so I'm not sure I really trusted him anyway. So I decided to stick with the little I knew about being a stewardess so I had an answer when people asked me what I wanted to be. I didn't know much else, and my parents from Germany did not understand higher education in this country…yet.

My mom worked at an accounting firm as a tax accountant and secretary. She loved her co-workers and they valued her and promoted education, so they gave her the name of a reputable counselor to help me find a career path in college. He was expensive but always overbooked so we felt lucky he saw me right away.

I entered his old, musty, paneled office, filled with diplomas on the wall and books everywhere. He was a thin and frail older man with wiry gray hair, and sharply focused eyes. He sat behind a large mahogany desk, which he looked up from, after he told us to come in. His voice was commanding, deep, and intelligent. He made eye contact with us, smiled, and guided us to where to sit down.

"Let's get right to it," he began. "Tell me about yourself."

He asked us questions, followed by more detailed questions, and winding down with "Name three books you've read recently," and "What is your favorite book?"

I looked down after this long interview, and without a flinch stated, "The Bible.". We were all somewhat tired, so my answer woke everyone up, though I could not believe those words came from my mouth. I didn't read but a little of the Bible in Sunday school so where did that come from. I believe it was just God just tapping me on the shoulder, to remember I could ask.

Anyway, the counselor initially suggested marketing, design, and liberal arts as the best possible career choices for me.

We went home and I sat at the kitchen table after dinner, which was always healthy. We ate foods such as kale, which I half fed to my dog under the table. I knew I had to make a decision about school, particularly since I was a late applicant. At first I agreed to marketing because I was very creative. Then everyone else left the kitchen after doing the dishes. I sat at the kitchen table, dimmed the kitchen lights, and breathed in the quiet evening. It was 9 o'clock; the cuckoo clock sang.

I sat remembering the place...the absolute truth and beauty and love... Remembering I could pray and ask.

I folded my hands, bowed my head, and prayed. I talked about all my concerns, specifically and clearly. I felt the connection, and kept praying until I felt myself open completely and sincerely. I asked for guidance and stated that I would open the book of careers the counselor had given me, and ask God to help me pick the best one for me. I would close my eyes and whichever career path my finger landed on would be the one I would trust and choose.

As I closed my eyes and opened the book, I felt complete faith and peace. I turned to a page that my gut instinct felt was right and I felt the peace of divine guidance. I believed my gut feeling was under His care, and after praying, I moved my finger down the page. "Nope, that one's not right," and continued turning pages until my guided instinct felt right about where to stop. My finger landed firm and still, completely planted in one spot. I prayed again: "Okay, I am trusting this is the spot. I will open my eyes and embrace it."

When I opened my eyes, I discovered my finger was on "nursing," something I never thought I would do. But I was sure because I knew only one thing mattered: the strongest trusted answer from the right source. So it was a done deal because of this prayer. I would be a nurse.

The comedy hour came when I told my family. "A nurse? She can't eve clean out a turkey at thanksgiving without getting squeamish," my mom said. Those in the neighborhood made bedpan jokes. Everyone figured since I was "beautiful" on the outside, I would have chosen a more glamorous career path, such as modeling or dancing. Despite Otto's values, my mom had sent me to modeling school, where I learned how to apply makeup, how to dress, and how to walk a runway. I actually walked the runway for a tuxedo company that did shows for school proms. I received a free tuxedo for the guy I would go to prom with. Most guys didn't have much money at that age, so it was helpful. Since I didn't really have anyone special in mind at the time, I decided to give the free tuxedo to a friend.

After modeling school, I received a portfolio of me wearing different outfits and makeup. I didn't feel comfortable with the photographer snapping pictures of me, though, but it gave me the reinforcement and experience I needed to choose to use my brain instead of my looks. Obtaining a science degree and serving others as a nurse seemed a better fit. Besides, I figured I'd be more comfortable around other compassionate healing people. My dad defended my choice because he had always believed in me. He gave me a million compliments and confidence boosts. What a supportive man.

In the end, I let the light guide my path, and didn't open it up for anyone to question. Plus, it was a practical choice because I would always have a job somewhere. So despite my mom's confusion, she supported it with a smile, and said "okay."

Later she told me she never thought I would stick to it. She was at my graduation, very impressed and proud, as nursing school exposed me to some of the most difficult situations possible. I nearly gave up many times and continued on because I trusted in the divine guidance. In times when I felt like a complete failure, I prayed for strength, and got it. We were a team. My mother's belief that I had a special connection and she could too continued to grow.

I picked the university in the same manner. Every time I visited a school, I chose to ask for help and guidance and trusted that God would let me know if I was in the right place. I liked the peace it brought. I always asked Him to give me a sign and for me to be able to trust my gut. It was fun. It was a mystery to figure out sometimes. It filled me with wonder and light. I was guided and decided to choose a small school in Westchester, New York, which even had a farm on the property.

The nursing program was very intense. I studied the hardest in my first two years. At the end of the four years, only about half my class graduated. Nursing school was very strict. We had to be on time and if we missed more than two clinical classes, we failed the course. One woman had a heart attack and another girl's father died. Both failed. My dad said if I quit school after two years, get my associates degree and he'd buy me a Camaro, or I could finish the program and get my bachelor's degree. I decided education can never be taken away, and if I ever wanted to change careers I could get my master's degree in something else. I finished my associates degree in science and nursing and because it was an accelerated program I was able to take my registered nurse state board exam at an early age of 19, which I passed. I continued for the next two years and completed my B.S.N.

In my forties I became a nursing instructor and saw the program hadn't changed. It was still very demanding. Even though I complained about the hard work sometimes, the rewards were amazing. It was meaningful to teach future healers and care givers. I lost track of myself completely while working, listening to others problems, and planning patient care. Sometimes I saw things that made me wonder why certain people even ended up under my care, people who took perfectly good care of them and got terrible illnesses anyway. But I also saw a few miracles, the power of the human spirit, spiritual power that had no scientific explanation that we could see. It is a very grounding profession. I saw at times how the light worked through people who were trying to help and heal others.

CHAPTER 24

MAYA DIES: THE PHONE CALL

While working at the medical center the year before I left for vacation to Florida, I got the call my mother said all her life she could never survive, the call that Maya had died. I received the call from Germany when no one else was home. I dreaded telling my mom, so I asked God for strength and He gave it to me. Upon hearing the news, however, she had a breakdown and needed medication. Her pain was excruciating, the stress of a broken heart. I felt a lot of grief, but held it back because my mother was so upset. I knew Maya loved me and I her. We were good. She had been a shell of her previous self after Otto died, visited him every day at his grave, and lived alone. One day when she was visiting his grave, a thug raped her.

She walked home freezing cold in the winter, went to bed, and no one saw her until she got pneumonia. Maya would wrap herself in blankets and try to sweat it out. She wouldn't go see a doctor because she was afraid to leave the house after the attack. So the pneumonia took over and she soon died.

So I went on vacation to Florida. It was beautiful, warm, and sunny: flip flops and suntans, sand, the clear blue waters of the ocean, the waves rolling in, and the peace of sitting at the beach. How I loved to swim. My friend Maureen said, "Why don't you move here? We can be roommates."

I thought, *Wow, if I work 3 p.m. to 11 p.m. I can go to the beach every morning.* So I went home with the idea in my head. When I got home it was snowing hard because it was February. I bet you can guess how I decided to move to Florida. Well this time I decided to move because of the snow, but I did have my special talks with God and dialed the phone to Heaven again.

My last day of work, it was snowing especially hard. The snow was accumulating faster than the plows could remove it. On my last day of work at the medical center, I got to dig Rooney out of the snow one last time in the dark after finishing the late night shift in the cardiac unit. I was a cardiac nurse, so I had seen many medical broken hearts and the effects of too much stress. I learned that stress, loss, and heartache could actually kill you. I also learned some of the spiritual power of the heart, witnessed people's spirits waiting for the arrival of a newborn baby, or to say goodbye to a loved one before he or she passed.

In the 1980s, I actually saw the first open-heart surgery at the medical center, which lasted eight hours. I saw doctors use streptokinase to stop an active heart attack while it was happening. We had a progressive medical center. Some of our interns played football on their days off. We worked as a team for the best care we could give. And I never saw a person who was dying who wished they had one more day at work, that they had been more successful, or that they had more money. Instead they regretted not being able to spend more time with a loved one, not being able to make peace with someone they'd had fallout with, or missing the opportunity to see future loved ones born.

In the end, we care about love. We worry about loved ones. We don't care about material things or how we look to others. I saw the will of the human spirit to live when inspired by love, and I saw those who had no real love in their lives and gave up because they were lonely; they had no one to live for. Medicines are for the vehicle, the physical body; love is for the spirit; and a positive attitude is for the mind. All are need for a healthy life.

CHAPTER 25

THE MOVE TO FLORIDA

The night before I planned to move to Florida, I drove to New York to visit my ex-boyfriend Chris to get closure. He professed his love for me, after I'd found two empty champagne glasses on his nightstand not too many weekends before. He had always been so faithful, so what was this? I wanted more than that, but in the moment I really wanted him back despite the red flags. So, knowing I needed help, I dialed the phone to Heaven and prayed.

Chris invited me to stay and wanted us to get back together, but I explained I was moving to Florida the following morning. When we left his place, I really didn't know what I was going to do. I followed his yellow Camaro and asked Jesus to guide me. I had no idea what would happen; I just knew I had to remain sincere and trust completely. The next morning, I drove behind Chris when he left for work. If I turned onto the highway to get home, I would take that as a "no" and if I followed Chris to his office, I would take that as a "yes."

It was so hard because I really did want to stay with him. When the exit approached, I saw Chris' face looking at me in his rear-view mirror. Then a strong calm and peace came over me, and I completely let go and let God. I said "Jesus take the wheel." When

I came to the exit, he slowed down and waited, hoping I would choose to stay. After I paused, trying to stay, an energetic whoosh of something came over me. I turned my blinker on, stepped on the gas, took the exit ramp, and did not look back. I felt as if my body was not my own as I watched with just as much surprise as Chris had. It felt like an out-of-body experience. It was really about completely letting go and letting God. I drove free as a bird, heart-broken in a way, but sure that I was being guided down the right path. I didn't like it, but I knew I was being helped with heartache. I headed home to New Jersey for one more night before the big move to Florida.

CHAPTER 26

THE LOVING PARTNER PRAYER

That night I went out for a while and ran into some old high school friends. One was the boy from kindergarten I used to sit next to, I was excited to see them, but heartbroken and knowing I promised to move to Florida in the morning I said my goodbyes. This was a crossroad and choice. I returned home and I sat in my bedroom feeling so hurt and said a prayer in my bed while sobbing. I will always remember that moment. I finally prayed and asked for help to find a heart that would truly love me. I found later when doing this it might be a good idea to be as specific and detailed as you can. Try not to leave out anything important to you.

So, I packed up my maroon Subaru, which I named "Rooney," and with youth on my side I set out to find new adventures in sunny Florida to meet my friend Maureen.

As I drove off in the morning, I looked in my rearview mirror and saw my mom running behind me in the road toward my moving car, covering her mouth of screams with her hand, trying not to collapse in the street as she saw me pull away from her. She was so upset. I knew she was happy for me, so she forced a smile and forced her feet to stop dashing like a squirrel in the road. She was waving as I drove off. I honestly could not feel all her pain because

I wasn't a mom yet. Plus I had my own heartache to deal with, so I looked at the move as a pain reliever.

I looked back and kept driving, knowing I would call her that evening, even though we didn't have cell phones then. Today I look back at that day, and see that I ran, not from her, but toward something else. I ran from the familiar surroundings, the places that held memories that tied me to Chris. Funny thing was, when I got to Florida they were still there. The pain was to a better level and distractions helped, but moving didn't change the heart.

Florida had its own challenges. It wasn't all fun and games, but it had room for that. Maureen and I found an apartment and we knew for sure we would get along because we lived together in college. Somehow just being around Maureen was so awesome, relaxing, and fun. We were excited about our own apartment, even though we did not have a stitch of furniture. I had a budget and was waiting to start my new job at a hospital in Florida in a few days. In the meantime, we shopped at a place that hires recovering alcoholics and drug addicts to build furniture and sells it for a small profit. We bought a couch for $25, a coffee table for $10, along with lamps and a kitchen table. It was starting to feel like home.

We were happy to see the men and women recovering from addictions working. Some of the oak kitchen tables they made were gorgeous. If I hadn't asked, I never would have known it was a place for recovering addicts. It was operated very professionally, and the church did a great job of giving them a fishing pole rather than just a fish every day to eat.

Florida was so pretty, the palm trees and the sunsets. The warm air seemed to make people feel healthier, able to move their joints better than they would if they lived in the colder regions of the States. They have a saying in Florida: "Drive carefully; watch out for the snowbirds." People who could barely see over the steering wheel were called "dreaded low heads." Being a senior is a gift and a blessing because not everyone has the privilege to grow old. There was a large population of seniors, most of who were still driving even in their very old age. Eating out was very affordable if you went to the early bird specials.

Feeling like a fish out of water at times, missing my family, I went with a new friend to a soccer game in the park and drank some wine. In the heat of Florida, it's easy to get dehydrated and I got very tipsy. That night I also pushed myself to go to the home of some new friends, Colleen and Dave, because I'd promised to go earlier in the week. Colleen said she had someone she would like me to meet, and felt we would make a good couple. I wanted to back out because I was not sure I was ready to meet anyone new. But with much encouragement from friends, I went.

I went to the apartment building and rang Colleen's doorbell. The door opened and much to my surprise a tall, well-dressed man in white pants, a light blue-and-white-striped shirt, and nice shoes answered the door. He was very handsome and handed me a single red rose as I entered the apartment. Was this a dream? I never expected this. I smiled and thanked him, and then hid out in the kitchen. Colleen came in to the kitchen and we talked and giggled. Then she suggested I sit on the couch beside him. I declined and stayed in the kitchen. I was too nervous; he was gorgeous. Greg started to wonder why I was behaving in such an odd way. We all finally sat at the table and the chicken dinner was served.

We chatted and went to a night club to go dancing. Before getting in his car I joked, "How much money do you make? And what kind of car do you drive?" I remembered Colleen saying he was looking for a girl who was not going to ask those questions. He was tired of meeting girls who seemed to want man for his wallet. He was looking for a natural girl who would not be superficial. I was floored at what a gentleman he was. I never know what the next moment in life holds. Meeting someone special happened in the blink of an eye for me. Was this divinely guided? Was he the answer to my prayers?

At the night club, a Barbie doll plastic-looking waitress in a skimpy outfit passed by me and made a fuss over Greg knowing her, so I thought he might be a player. I went to the ladies' room and found within the crowd a friend I used to babysit with, named Michelle, from New Jersey. A Bruce Springsteen song came on and my New Jersey-girl confidence started to return. She mentioned a young man who had a crush on me in high school, and it reminded me I was attractive to some. I reentered the dance floor, found Greg, and we danced. He was a good dancer, but I still wondered whether he was a player. We went to the bar area and sat with Colleen and Dave, and I put some ice down his back in silly fun. He reacted calmly and smiled. We drove home, not knowing what to make of it all. Was there a connection? While driving, I began to sing to the radio, and he joined in comfortably. The tension broke and relaxed and accepting, comfortable smiles emerged. We connected by being ourselves a little bit. When we got back to my place, he walked me to my apartment and shook my hand goodnight. That never happened before.

I forgot about him until I had a flat tire at work and realized I did not have my family or any other male friends, so I called Greg. We went out after work, at which time I would usually be in a very hard and emotionally turned-off mode, until I could unwind. He told me a story about how he had lots of athletic scholarships to colleges, until he tore his knee playing football, which left him unable to walk and his dreams shattered. A very good surgical sports medicine team that also treated the Cleveland Browns treated him. He had surgery but was not expected to walk again. Eventually, though, he did walk again and has been walking perfectly ever since.

He walked me back to the apartment and shook my hand goodnight. But we spoke tense and uncomfortable words. I was just in a "mood," leftover from work at the hospital and didn't realize I'd been rude to him. Maureen overheard and when I came inside she said, "I hope you call him right away and apologize. I have never heard you be so rude to someone. That's uncalled for to treat someone that way." I didn't want to, nor did I care, but to save my friendship with Maureen, I did. He said he never would have spoken to me again if I hadn't made that phone call.

We forgot about each other, until the 4th of July when I was invited to party on the beach and Greg was there. We talked, comfortably surprised by our chemistry, relieved, and at peace. That night we talked by the ocean and connected.

We spent every day together after that. We went to buy tires together, shopped for groceries, cooked, and watched TV. One day I said I was going to the Bahamas on my weekend off for $69 round trip. Greg wanted to join. I said, "Please don't get any ideas to propose or anything; it is just a weekend trip together." I had filled out papers to be a traveling nurse in the Air Force Reserve. My original goal was to acquire real estate, travel, and open a Swiss bank account. I worked hard to be independent and secure in my work; I asked nothing from anyone.

After we got to the Bahamas, one night he proposed marriage. I was stunned. I wanted to stall, and asked, "What if I need more time?"

He said, "You either know or you don't. It's that simple.

It made sense, so I said "yes." I liked his direct approach. He did not have a ring, but I did not mind. Off we went to the casino where we won $75 and celebrated with a fancy dinner.

Returning home, I phoned my mom and told her the news. She had never heard of him before now, so she was shocked and went wild with motherly concern. "Who is he?" she frantically asked. "What is his name? Where is he from? What does he do for a living?"

I didn't know the answers to all of her questions, so I simply replied, "Mom, I would marry him even if he was a garbage man. He just feels right to me."

My mother and father were on the next plane, still wondering, "Who is this man?" It was not like me to make a decision before collecting all the information I needed. I chose to trust in the answer to my prayer.

CHAPTER 27

THE WEDDING

We were married in a small pink Florida chapel. It was so pretty. I washed my hair, put it in a ponytail, and applied a little makeup. When the wedding song played, I did not go out at first, so the pianist repeated it. My dad patiently waited, as I had cold feet, and escorted me out the second time the wedding march played. Ten people were in attendance. One person had no shoes and a lizard on his shoulder. The photographer Greg hired did not show, which was a little nerve racking.

We ate at a restaurant in a hotel on the beach that had a seafood buffet, glass sliding doors that opened to a full ocean view, and a band every weekend. They made a cake for us and we dined and danced. The first song the band played was "Push Push in the Bush," Calypso style. I was so embarrassed that I was blushing.

Our parents did not get along too well. Greg's parents spoke of getting us our own McDonald's restaurant, and we later found they could not. So my mother became concerned that I would not be used to people who did not follow through on promises. I was raised that if you didn't have it, you didn't offer. So it was disappointing to get our hopes up. The money his mother spent shopping for things like dolls, clothes, jewelry, and collectibles also made my parents uncomfortable. My mother believed that once you become a parent your children's needs come before yours. It seemed to be money squabbles between them; we left it between them, as they were adults. We promised to never put it between each other. Greg was a self-made man, and his parents left him to figure things out on his own and they were proud of that. They loved Greg very much and in their own way. I have always greatly appreciated and admired them for raising a good son.

Greg and I got along well, however; we respected each other and I knew he was a good man. He valued what I had achieved at an early age, and made me feel beautiful, happy, and peaceful inside. I valued his strong, clean mind and also many of his virtues. He was a very accomplished athlete and he was also a very handsome looking guy, especially in his baseball uniform. While we were at the pool one day, he said, "I promise I will never hurt you, and I will never leave you." Those were magic words for me, as if a skeleton key had turned and unlocked my heart.

Greg had a strong work ethic. He began working for McDonald's, as a kid, and had a genius-level IQ, and a chess champion. He made a steady paycheck and paid his own bills, so what he did for a living didn't matter to me. Plus, he treated me like a lady. He didn't curse, drink, or smoke. He treated me as precious and never belittled or made fun of me. He made me feel as if I was the most beautiful and cherished woman in the world, safe and protected. When he took me on dates, he paid and opened car doors. I knew we could build an honest future together.

On our honeymoon, he lost his wedding ring in the ocean, so I sometimes joke that I'm married to the sea. When we returned from Hawaii, we used the wedding money given so kindly by our parents for a down payment on a townhouse. We both worked the same jobs, but soon we started looking at owning a McDonald's restaurant. As I mentioned earlier, his parents thought they could assist, but were unable to. So I sold Rooney, my Subaru, and invested every dollar I made into the restaurant.

We ended up not purchasing one, but later we bought two truck-stop restaurants. I worked at those, plus the hospital. The HIV virus hit South Florida and I was stuck with a needle from someone I thought might be infected. The reality of my job hit me when I was pregnant with my son. So I began working less at the hospital and decided to be around Greg and the business more.

My mother had been in and out of pain clinics for a botched surgery on her spine and lung. Nerves were damaged, as doctors thought she had cancer, and she was left with daily life-long pain. It was so bad that doctors said they would have understood if she had taken a bottle of pills and ended it all. She was in Long Island, getting experimental treatment she heard worked for celebrities. One day she phoned me and said the treatment wasn't working and she actually did want to end her life.

I remember sitting on top of the laundry in my closet with the phone and crying after we hung up. I sat up night after night on the floor, looking out the sliding glass doors while Greg was sleeping, and looked at the moon. Thinking of Hedy, tears rolling softly down my left cheek, I prayed for her because I had so much compassion for what she was going through. Eventually I realized how much her condition affected all who loved her, so I made an effort to check on my brother more and tell my dad that I realized he must have been hurting so much, too. Soon after, she got breast cancer and felt pretty beaten down. She never gave up, though, and I noticed she began to privately read daily prayers and inspirational affirmations that were uplifting. She got comfort and strength from them. She kept them by her bedside tucked in her top drawer.

CHAPTER 28

THE GIFT OF BABIES

What an honor and a privilege to raise children. I felt how much Jesus loved His children and wouldn't it be great if everyone began by loving their own. We learn so much about loving someone and putting the needs of others before our own. My pregnancy was normal, except my girth was large enough for twins. Instincts I never knew I had began to developed as a mother, and a new intuition and a connection of pure protection out of deep love. I worked during the pregnancy until I could no longer. Labor was calculated to be February 14, the day my mom had survived her lung and spine surgery. I like to notice the dates and I do not really believe in coincidences.

I went into the beginnings of labor curiously on January 19, the day I survived the skiing accident. So whom is this person coming into the world with such impeccable timing? Gregory was born with his arm in the air, making a fist of victory! Indeed, he is a champion in our lives in every sense of the word. His mere arrival brought us all so much excitement for the future. He was a miracle in every way. Life is a miracle, so being part of bringing another into the world is a miracle, an honor and a blessing of the highest regard. Gregory carries the name of his father and the initial of both his grandpas. He was our first born and made us a family of our own so we passed on names as we considered it traditional.

When Gregory was two, he asked if he could pick a baby from the baby room, and he did. Out of all the babies, he picked Eric. It was interesting that he was born on the same day as my good friend, Maureen, so Eric and Maureen are birthday buddies. It was St. Patrick's Day, and I don't believe this is a coincidence. What an interesting an extraordinary day to be born. He is just as extraordinary. Although we are not Irish as far as I know, we now shared a connection to St. Patrick and the history of that day through Eric's birth! Eric was easy going, calm, flexible, and happy as long as he could see me nearby. Eric gave me the feeling of peace and delight. His name means prince and he carries the name perfectly. A celebration fills our hearts for the arrival of Eric! He added so much love and light to our family. I appreciated each child as a gift and treated them as individuals who passed through me, and me respectfully had their own life lessons and journey to travel. I was committed to support and nourish whatever their individual unique person needed and watching that miracle grow. Children can teach us so much, and remind us how to find our way back when we get lost in the world. They truly are a gift and a blessing.

I fell deeply in love again with this new life, and the two boys now had me all to themselves, as we couldn't afford day care if we wanted to. Greg made a good living, though, and I made sure I spent every second I could loving my children, enjoying them, and caring for their needs. Although I saw others careers take off and have more money than us, sometimes I wished I had, but it does not compare to spending time with them, and I will never regret spending my time with my children. It is a great privilege and joy.

The gift of being a parent gave me the opportunity to love someone more than myself and to learn to put someone before myself. God's love for His children was even more understood after becoming a parent.

Christine… a strong girl on a mission; she really wanted to be here. I tell her birth story in detail because it was a time when I was told I could no longer have children, and I hope it brings hope to others. The pregnancy after a ruptured ectopic was touch and go, but an amazing doctor built and reinforced my faith and trust in medicine again. Christine gave me a feeling of being young, healthy, and renewed. She healed the wound of the ruptured ectopic.

I never thought I could have another baby especially since I only had some of my reproductive parts. The boys were so curious and so happy, wondering as children do, how Christine would affect their lives. One night I was home, feeling huge and like a hermit, when a friend called to ask me out for a bite to eat. I was grumpy and tired during my last trimester of pregnancy, and she was running late. So when she finally called around 7 p.m., the reputation I had for being sweet went out the window. I said "Forget it; it's late and I'm not going out. I don't want to sleep on a full stomach." She panicked and begged but I felt she was inconsiderate of my condition. She wouldn't leave me alone, she kept coming by the house, and by this point, and I was aggravated.

We arrived at the home of another friend, Miriam, and I thought, *Oh great, another delay. Don't they know I'm pregnant, tired, and due to deliver soon?* I went inside Miriam's home to speed her up, and when I entered, I heard "Surprise!" at the volume of the football stadium, or a loud concert. Everyone I had ever known was there to celebrate this baby. A baby shower thrown by my mom and friends commenced in full spirit of joy! I was so shocked and surprised. I opened gifts while I was sitting with balloons behind my chair. I ate great food with friends and family, and went home high as a kite floating up in the sky.

That week I came down with the flu. I was in bed one evening, watching a chic flick, with tissues piled on top of my comforter and on the floor. I didn't want to move an inch. I felt exhausted just getting up and going to the bathroom. I looked down, and water was flowing down my leg, warm and clear. Confused for a second, I yelled, "Greg, my water broke!" He came rushing upstairs, and we went to the car. He was driving so fast the steering wheel shook. Greg managed to cut an hour's drive to thirty minutes.

Out came a wheelchair and in we went. Doctors examined me while I was trying to direct them in my bossy nurse take-charge tone. While I was barking orders for an epidural anesthesia only (no spinal), they agreed while injecting me with a spinal anyway and told me the baby was presenting transverse. Her shoulder was coming out first. So the spinal was given, and I was rushed to the operating room (and remember, this was all happening while I had the flu). I kept saying, "I'm not giving birth today. How in the world can I do this?" Well, I did.

The anesthesia and I didn't get along. I began to seize, and after the first cut came the words, "Whoa! She has the biggest plumbing I ever saw."

"Really?" I asked.

"Yes, the biggest ever. In all my years, I've never seen anything like this."

"Is that good?"

"Great for the baby, not so good for the mommy. We can't cut you open routinely. If we nick anything you will bleed out on the table and we won't be able to stop it."

So another incision was made, and again, "Stop; that was too close. We have to try another way."

They cut me from bikini line to navel and said the three cuts looked like the letter "L." It took a few hours to close it all up, but when she was born through all the non-stop seizing, I swore I would never complain about anything again. The doctors escorted Greg out, as he had felt light headed while he was witnessing all this. Christine was born, and I was rushed to the recovery room.

All I could think of was her eyes, her beautiful spirit, and the boys and their eyes. I was in recovery a long time. I was later placed in the closest bed to the nursing station, so I knew I was a high risk. They gave me bags of medicine intravenously, and I was in and out of consciousness, but when they brought me the baby, a high came over me. Shortly afterward, we went home and her brothers joined in the excitement in their own special ways.

I named her Christine...
Christ is in that name....

Her brothers were eleven and nine, and they now had a new baby sister. I had my hands full, keeping their sports life going without a kink while accommodating a newborn. I knocked myself out with hopes that they would never feel jealous that the baby took all my time, but I have no regrets about that. I gave them my entire all. My three children are my beautiful miracles. I loved paying attention to the details of their birthdates, names, times, and the way they entered the world. They each brought so much love.

Life became alive with us being a family of five now. I had never imagined being part of a big family and feel blessed.

CHAPTER 29

LOSS OF A LOVED ONE

We can all be more mindful and speak with compassion instead of quickly telling people to "get over it and move on." We are all trying. We can hold love for people in our hearts forever, and that is perfectly okay because love never ends. The following story gives us some beautiful insight for us all.

While I was working as a nurse at the hospital, a 98-year-old woman was a patient there. Walking with my coat on and my feet feeling the pain of a long day, I was rushing down the hall toward to exit when I heard a voice say, "Nurse." I looked around and saw the flickering of the fluorescent yellowing light bulbs coming from a room I passed, and once again I heard the faint cry of "Nurse." I turned around to the room that was dark with curtains drawn. I opened the curtains and in the dark I saw the small, frail 98-year-old woman. I turned on the soft bedside light and saw the pink curlers in her hair. She had rosy cheeks, white hair, and a wrinkled complexion. She smelled like rose water and was well cared for. She also had a sign above her bed that said she was legally blind.

She asked my name, and I told her "Susanne." Then she asked if I could help her. I sat at the edge of her bed and held her trembling hand. She asked if I could keep a secret, and promise not to tell anyone else, not even her family. Then she asked if I'd be her nurse and if I would come to her room every night.

So I worked to help her. She loved her husband, who she was married to for many years until he had passed away a few years before. She also loved her children, grandchildren, and great grandchildren. She read every night and asked me if I could reach in her drawer and pull out her Bible. When she was finished with it, she asked if I could put it back in the exact spot. She was always nervous and anxious about handling her Bible carefully.

She asked me if I would open it, which I did, and turn the pages until I found a piece of paper. It was yellow, handwritten, and looked old and tattered. She asked me to treat it very carefully.

"I need it to fall asleep every night," she said, "so could you be a dear and read it to me? I can't ask my family and I will tell you why later."

So I opened the letter, and she took a deep breath. "Okay I'm ready; you can begin."

It began "Dear…" followed by her name. As I read it, I realized it was a love letter from a man who was overseas during the war. She and this man had a life and dreams planned.

As I finished reading it to her, I said, "Wow, you saved the letter all these years."

She said, "Yes, but it was not from my husband." That's why she couldn't ask her family to read it to her. She loved them all very much and didn't want them to be hurt or confused and she did not want to degrade her husband's memory.

The letter was from a man she had loved and promised to marry, but he was shipped off to war. She waited for him to return but he was killed in action. "I kept him in my heart all these years," she said, "and I read his letter every night to fall asleep. I never forgot him, even though I loved my husband very much."

For the time being I agreed to keep her secret. I read the letter to her the next night, as well, and she fell asleep. She told me she slept very well and thanked me. After that night I never told another person who suffered a loss, to "get over it," nor have I ever put a time limit on someone else's grief. She kept that love in her heart all her life. She said there was room for more, and her heart was big enough for everyone she loved.

I believe accidents and tragedies happen, and they rarely make any sense, so we feel punished or abandoned by God. I certainly do not have all the answers, but His loving system and universe is not designed for us to be loved and give love, to be part of a family, to have children, only to be ripped apart forever by death. We are here to learn about love and grow in lessons of love. Accidents happen. We are responsible for the creation of pollution that causes sickness to our bodies, and some choose to create hate and destroy others or themselves. However, we never lose love and what is real. People who keep their light on, relight their tired light after they have suffered a tragedy are an inspiration and a help to others. People, who have suffered and continue to carry on, try a new road, or continue to give, are so beautiful.

Wouldn't it be nice to have a weekly rain of compassion from the sky, like divine water, to soothe us? If you've lost a loved one, I don't know why it happened, or why you're here and that person isn't, but having seen Heaven, I do know it is real. Maybe you're still here to impact the life of another you haven't met yet. Maybe you are the answer to someone else's prayer. There is a purpose to each of our lives. He will bring you understanding when He feels it is best. If you can just leave your light on simply by waking up every morning and facing the day, you are doing amazing. If you don't believe in anything, maybe you will in the future. Maybe you will live a good life and help others. You never know for what experience you are being prepared for. You are amazing just by keeping your light on.

CHAPTER 30

PREACHERS ARE HUMAN

Preachers can be inspirations. But there are good and bad in every profession, including preaching, so don't feel bad if you don't feel connected to every minister, priest, or preacher. . They are not to be confused with being God; they are merely people. They aren't any closer to Him than you or I.

Don't turn your back on your spirituality because you don't like the way someone preaches, or because you don't feel you fit in. Houses of religion always incorporate man's perspective, so decline it if your gut tells you to. Instead seek answers with guidance, and only invite pure light and love in prayer. Block all voices of darkness.

A preacher who preached once turned off my son about his personal judgments toward different cultural lifestyles. One Sunday he walked out and almost pulled away from his own religion, but I asked him instead to question the man's spiritual maturity and character. He did not want to return to church, and I told him maybe it was just that church he did not want to return to. We were new in the area, so we have since visited different churches and are choosing one. Information is only as good as its source, so beware of inviting the wrong information, the wrong people, and the wrong decisions into your life. I know that the universe is filled with love to draw upon, and that there are good people who carry light and love.

We can choose to step forward to help another when we notice someone is struggling. To the lovely person struggling, don't quit. Call someone; reach out. Once you're out of the crisis, try to keep your tank more than half full daily. Pray, take a walk, take a bath, light a candle, eat a good meal, read, notice nature's beauty, or just appreciate the wind on your face. You are alive, what a gift each day is. There is always something to appreciate: your eyesight, the sun, the rain, or a bird in a tree, your health or a day without pain. Keep looking, and if it all goes dark, get help, and allow yourself to receive it. If someone judges you, realize where he or she is in his or her learning to love.

Being a good friend can make an important difference in someone's life, as well. Call someone you know and ask, "How are you? How can I help?" Give a hug or a cooked meal, or just listen to someone else who is going through a crisis. It is good medicine and brings someone else to a better level of comfort. I'm always thankful for the moments someone else listened to me, and still looks at me with the same loving eyes because whatever it was I was going through did not change their view of or respect for me. So I try to do the same.

CHAPTER 31

LIFE'S PURPOSE

How many times have I heard people ask what their life's purpose is? Your life's purpose is simply to be yourself and to experience, learn, and share your gifts and love. Your life speaks your message to the world, so make it inspiring. Being your true self is so important. The freedom to truly be who you are is a gift to yourself and your life. Just be who you are truly are and share your special gifts. I lived with a secret to respect my mother. I honored her wishes. Today I see that in everything there is risk of ridicule and judgment. They stem from fear of the unknown. Though they exist and make it difficult, should it deter us from sharing our truths and gifts?

We are all special in some way. Survival is sometimes a journey we take. We are not all expected to receive the Nobel peace prize, or do monumental change the world in a day tasks. We can choose to practice making better choices daily. To chose to impact another's life in a positive way. We don't always get to see the rewards of being helpful, but we can trust that it is. We can get by without taking and hurting others. Being a good parent, working every day, sharing ourselves, and being good listeners are all important life purposes. Simply by being your authentic self and becoming the best version of yourself is a life's purpose. Live your life; survive the pitfalls; and appreciate the joys, the wonders, and the gifts such as a simple sunrise or a rose. All we have to do each day is wake up and decide how we are going to spend the next twenty-four hours. Every day is a new day, a new chance, and a gift. That's how much God loves us,

So share your stories, listen without speaking quickly, and look around at the wonders of nature, share the stories of your lives and families.

CHAPTER 32

BECOMING A FINANCIAL PROVIDER

Well, shortly after, Greg's position at work was "eliminated," even after he had made that company millions of dollars he was let go, purposely before the franchise owner paid him all money due for his services. It was no reflection of Greg. He did all the right things and took a sinking company and turned a tremendous profit winning awards. This was our children's college money, our retirement, and our security. We heard another member of the company contemplated suicide. Greed is so destructive. We were told by the owner not to take it personal its only business.

We all agreed there had been a decline in company values. What different times we live in so shortly after our parents' generation. Some think it is brilliant to save money and let seniors go before they get full retirement, requiring families to be separated with traveling most of the month. I remember when Otto received that Blue Max as an honor of longevity and dedication for his service at Mercedes Benz. Those in the next generation got a watch and a dinner and were let go before they were fully vested.

Seniors were once valued for time served in a company, but that has changed, forcing people to job hop when they should be retiring. Family values and good character have been lowered down the ladder of society to mean, "Nice guys finish last." Smart guys learn ways around the system and cheat people, while others think they're clever. But they are not smarter for cutting corners by cheating others, eliminating jobs, and having no morals when running companies.

I went back to school to renew my nursing skills while Greg tried to work from home, starting his own business. Christine was four; Gregory, fifteen; and Eric, thirteen. I had been running to all their sports games. Ice hockey became their focus and they were tops in it. I spent hours a day nursing a baby, and driving all over the East Coast for their dreams. Now I needed to pull my nursing license out of my back pocket of security. So I went to college to refresh my license and then got a job. Greg watched Christine at home while working, but he was on the computer often, so we eventually enrolled her in a childcare program. She would be there more and more, as I had to work long shifts to prove myself and make the needed income, while carrying the medical benefits for the family. It showed me education mattered. It bridged to save the day. Greg was always an excellent provider and continued immediately after to do so. It gave me an opportunity to teach my children the value of education.

I missed time with my children, knowing this was the most important and fulfilling work I could ever do. Unfortunately life and Maslow's hierarchy of needs sat me in my seat of providing food and shelter; work is never an option when you have a family. I became inspired, however, to show them love in this way. I was thankful for the ability to work.

I spent much time being grateful for what we did have. We all are given so much and are so loved. Counting my blessings is how I liked to try and start the day. Being a nurse I have seen how it can always be worse and how quickly that can happen. So I have developed a way to look for the good in situations, and look for the positive with genuinely sharing compassion. Surround yourself with positive thoughts and actions are a key to happiness.

CHAPTER 33

SHARING IMPRINTS FROM HEAVEN

"It is a good practice to make deposits along the way in life into your spiritual bank accounts to save for a rainy day." These are some of the practices I have used to fill my spiritual bank account along my journey.

GRATITUDE AND APPRECIATION

Taking a moment to notice something I do have instead of something I don't have. It is a daily practice and not to be left out in hard times. I learned to be grateful for a day without pain, or my legs working well, my hands able to work, and the love of those around me. If it is something I don't have maybe I can obtain, it, then it becomes a goal to work towards. I learned that limits are our own doing. I learned that how we look at things creates our life.

SEEING THE GOOD

Heaven gave me a strong sense of seeing the good in everybody and being kind to people who are hurt. I know there are people who say they have that too and for many years, I thought that was true. But later in life I came to realize that my seeing the good in everyone is extreme. Extremes can be dangerous and I had to do some work in this area to fit back into our society.

One evening when I was in my thirties, I was walking out of a store; a man approached me in the dark, grabbed me, and held a knife to my throat. I was alone and no one was around. I saw him approach from the side of the tall bushes that lined the walkway from the store to the parking lot. I handed the man my purse and he took it. I thought he was going to let me go, but I was wrong. He stood there in silence, and his hands were shaking. I broke the silence and said, "You have plenty of money in there. Go do what you need to do. I understand you must need it badly."

He stood back a bit and said, "What?"

I replied, "I understand; life can be hard on us all. I'm sure you have a very good reason for this."

He said, "Shut up."

I said, "Don't worry; the only thing I'll miss is a cigarette," and laughed a bit.

He took the knife away, allowed me to face him, and said, "Man, you are a strange lady."

I reached into my coat pocket and pulled out a cigarette, looking for a lighter. I then asked him, "Do you want a cigarette?" I began to talk about what a rough day it had been and began to start a conversation. I asked him "What's wrong?" and "Are you okay?"

He took a cigarette and I said, "Let's sit down a minute; I could use the company." We sat on the ground and smoked a cigarette. He handed me my purse to look for the lighter. I handed him the purse back. We talked and he told me his life story. I hugged him. He hugged me back. He was a drug addict. Still shaking, he handed me the purse back, apologized, and said, "I need help." I gave him another hug. I gave him the cash and asked if I could keep the "girl junk" in my purse.

He said, "Sure."

As I was going to ask if I could drive him to the hospital, he began to get agitated again. I knew it was time to move on, so I said, "I need to get home, but I want you to know you are loved. God loves you and so do I, and I will pray for you."

He looked confused and rubbed his hair. He said, "I don't know why," then paused for a minute, and continued, "but I believe you." He said he would try to better although he didn't think it was possible.

I said, "I'll try to do better too; we all should," and smiled.

Our eyes locked and a grin emerged between us, no words, but a long look that said so much. Our hearts connected and he said, "Have a good night special lady," and we walked away in different directions, with him running after he had taken a few steps. I walked at a regular pace so I wouldn't trigger more anxiety in him, got in my car, and went straight home.

When I got home, I was calm and happy and excited as I told the story to Greg. He sat quiet and frozen. He began shaking his head. He said, "I don't know how you got so lucky, and yet I do." I saw the good in that man.

There are a many stories like this one that happen every single day; I can share just a few.

There was a man in the hospital, who was throwing his dishes at the nurses and calling them names. The nurses were crying when he attacked them, and that's saying a lot, considering nurses are trained psychologically to understand the potential outbursts of anger as part of the Kubler –Ross stages of grief. So the nurses took turns entering this man's room, but eventually no one wanted to go in. I offered to take him as a patient. "Fine," said my coworkers, as they turned their backs to me and scurried off busily as if to hurry away before I changed my mind. He was middle-aged and in the later stages of MS, so he was wheelchair bound, watching his body deteriorate from the legs up. The MS had begun to spread to his chest area, so he feared it would affect his heart.

Yes, he threw things at me, and refused to allow us to check his blood sugar. He made fun of me, and mocked me, and tried everything to run us all away. I told him as I took him to the bathroom one day, and he was angry to need my help, that he was more that just his disease. There was a long silent pause. He took a deep breath and said, "Yes I am."

I told him he was handsome, smart, and a good dad. Then I asked him what he wanted to be known for in the end. This disease? Would he let this disease define him completely? Would he become the disease? "You are so much more than this disease," I said.

Day after day I let him have his outbursts and made a game out of checking his blood sugar with him in control. He desperately needed control since the MS had stolen so much from him. So I gave him control and reminded him we are not here to force anything on him, just to help. He could refuse anything, and go home and he could tell us all to go to H-E-double hockey sticks, but he got quieter and quieter. One day upon laughing together, he said, "You are a funny lady. You didn't bang down the front door; you came in through the back door and helped me see the light."

I reminded him of how loved he is and that he is a unique person in the world. I asked him if he wanted to get a cup of coffee together. I took him in his wheelchair to the cafeteria and we got our coffees. Then we went outside for some fresh air, drank the coffee and watched the snow fall. He said I was his Christmas angel, and he will never forget that moment of awakening. We held hands for a moment. He said his personal faith in more than just his disease was renewed, and he phoned his daughter that night and told her he loved her after many years of silence between them. She gave him a happy and tearful response. He smiled so big his teeth could blind you.

He said he would always remember that night no matter where he was. He said he would remember the moment in his darker hours. I told him I would too, and I have.

Other nurses took him as a patient again and this time he was teasing them and complimenting them.

He joked as I saw him in the mornings out in the hall in his wheelchair, shouting "Good morning!" day after day to patients passing by. He became known as "the mayor of the hospital" since he was lifting people's spirits by talking and greeting everyone he passed with a smile, a "good morning," and a compliment. We all have the choice to impact others in a good way, and it has a ripple effect. It grows love.

My family felt seeing the good in people was dangerous for me at times, as I would not be able to see the bad. They were right but over time they knew I wasn't stupid and not learning to be safer, I was just not able to see it. I would joke that I'm missing that chip; I dropped it on the way to Heaven. I can't explain it any other way than the imprints of my visit to Heaven. When I see the good in someone, they are reminded to see the good in themselves.

I see the good in those who everyone else ignores or has given up on. I can't help but see it, and more than that, tell them what I see, with no expectations but to give them the reminder they are alive and loved. It is so gratifying to not be so self-important to forget that we are all connected. More and more I see a movement of people to be more aware of others around them and that giving is so rewarding.

As a person who experienced so much love from Heaven, and a person who became a nurse to help others, I had an extremely hard time ever giving up on anyone in pain. Impossible for me to do, but I had to learn boundaries later in life and let go to protect myself and stay away from danger. I can do it, but I really feel like the last man standing. I don't want to call the "code" until there is absolutely no hope at all. So that is a big part of my experience of seeing the afterlife. I have gotten hurt, but I continue.

We can see the good in people by being aware of the people around us, by looking at body language and facial expressions, and reaching out when we see someone who looks down, or someone who doesn't. Just take notice of a nice-looking sweater or pay a random compliment on someone's hair, shoes, smile, or their contagious laugh. See the good in another's smile, appreciate a door opened, and say "thank you" when someone does something thoughtful, helpful, and nice for you, to let them know it made you feel good. We first see the good but it's great if we take the step to letting the person know we see it. Taking notice of someone can make that person's day.

We can see the good in situations and recognize how much we can avoid confrontation by the way we communicate. There are great tools to learn to speak to people and not put each other on the defensive. One thing we can do to disarm others is to let people know you want to like them, you want to get along, and you are trying to do so. If you disagree, respect another's opinion as his or her own. God gave us our free will and loves us unconditionally. His seeing the good is so much more than I could ever describe, or fully know, but in Heaven that great love is undeniable, unwavering, and all-loving.

In Heaven I saw the light in beings, the beauty of its love, the goodness inside that radiates through and shines so bright, the comfort of it. Remembering the good in us is important too. Isn't it funny how people can do so many good things for each other and then one wrongdoing destroys it all? I know it depends on the wrongdoing; however, it is mystifying when it is just a misunderstanding, and many times it is. I don't usually give up until I have to. Even then I pray for enlightenment and change for the good of the situation, for better understanding of the other person, to try to realize I have not walked in his or her shoes. Since Heaven, I have been mocked for giving people a million chances and new starts. I seem to not be wired to truly give up on finding peace and seeing the good, or do everything I can to heal or lead to healing.

There is undying and unconditional love for us, all day, every day. We are all connected and we all have a purpose. When we help another, we help ourselves. When we hurt another we hurt ourselves. It is a gift to have a life. When we don't learn life's lessons, another opportunity will come up, and the cycle will continue to repeat until the lesson is learned. We are all a work in progress. Seeing the good in someone is like seeing a piece of the light and love of God.

There is good and bad, or shall I say, "challenging" in everything. At times I have felt so alone in this amazing experience, missing the kind of connections I experienced in the afterlife. Sometimes when trying to connect with people, I can believe they are sincere, caring, and dialed in, but somewhere along the line some sort of ego, need to one up or compete, judge others, insecurity, fear, or some other negative sets in. I miss the purity of heart I witnessed, the understanding. Sometimes when people just live in their heads it confuses their heart. It is part of each person's journey to find the mind and heart connection. It is part of our journey to forgive and understand where some might be in their journey.

So there is a choice we can all make in our lives. We can choose to make a positive change. Sometimes by taking one baby step and trying something simple and new, we find exactly what we felt was missing. Often loneliness is cured by just reaching out and helping someone else. I have also found in times of loneliness that it has become okay; maybe it is a time to focus and devote more time on self love and care to prepare for life's next adventure. Although we are very loved by Spirit, we also benefit greatly to have human contact, as infants do, to survive. To love each other and share physical touch is very powerful and it will add light to ourselves as we light and warm another's spirit. I list a few healing and uplifting messages that I brought back with me.

LAUGHTER

We all know how much we all love laughing and sharing a laugh together. It alleviates so much tension and uplifts the spirit.

Laughter is proven to be so healing. We are naturally drawn to those who make us feel good and laugh. It is an absolute gift some people have when they can make others laugh and smile with a funny story or a quick witted remark. It is a gift to have a good sense of humor. It helps others forget their problems and lighten up. Laughter somehow makes hard times not so overwhelming and more manageable. It reminds me not to take things so seriously. Often we find the humor in our worries with laughter and a great sense of humor. If you have this gift of bringing laughter you are spreading light and laughter and because it is so contagious!

MUSIC

The universal language of music carries a most high universal vibration. It is agreed that it can bring us instantly to a certain place and time, and has been spoken of as a high form of communication. When I worked in a neurological unit with brain injuries it was amazing how people had injured memories, but when we played songs they could remember the lyrics or melody. Music has so many moods and flavors. Some is healing, calming, or energizing. Take time to see how different music styles affect you during different moods and there are so many songs to choose from. I love instruments from all around the world. Lyrics and melodies can bring emotions to the forefront, helps us feel something, and create a validation that someone else has felt it too. They play music to an infant in the womb and have studied its benefits. Creating music is a wonderful gift to have and to share. Singing is so good for our soul. Humming also is a great thing to do when I am in an uncomfortable situation, or to break away from the negative words from someone else. Humming is a special secret. It has the ability to break the negative vibrations. I would sing or hum when I didn't want someone else's hurtful comments to affect my energy and outlook. .

THE RADIO GAME

I had a game I invented and played as a girl and I called it the radio game. It wasn't to make big life decisions; it just brought me spiritual comfort and support. So as a girl I listed to the radio and played this game. Here are the rules. I sat quiet and took a deep breath and turned the radio off. I bowed my head and closed my eyes. Sometime I had my eyes open and looked to the sky. I cleared my mind and this part may takes a few minutes to make sure the mind is clear from everything. The radio game won't work with an insincere or closed heart; it works with an open heart that has let go of doubt and trusts. Next I prayed and asked God my one question. It had to be a yes or no kind of question. I would then ask Him to send me a sign through the next song that came on the radio. I would only ask up to three questions that day. I turned on the radio and pressed the station I felt was the right one. I then turned on the volume. When it was a commercial, I waited for the next available song. If the song were almost over, I would listen and see if it has something in it that resonated with me. If it didn't resonate I believed no answer at that time is an answer. I asked God to give me a message through the radio and through the song. It was so much fun! I was never too young or old to play the radio game. I could feel when the message was for me. If there was confusion then I discounted it. Sometime there was static so I would know that the answer was not meant to come through right now. When I asked and paid attention the messages always came if they were meant to.

LOVE

Love is our greatest gift and all we ever take with us. It can create change. It has the power to heal, uplift, inspire and create. We are created by love. We create more love with love. We live life and learn so many ways to love and to improve and open our hearts. We live life to find a loving connection to God to fill our spirit.

Although at times in our life journey we feel loves keen sting from one another, spiritual love will never hurt you and always help you. We spend time learning how to heal the wounds from one another. During those times it is important to practice self love and begin healing by surrounding yourself with those who love you. To love one another doesn't mean that you continue to stay when being abused. Dust off your sandals and let go and let God. Walk away from anything that is hurting your spirit and causing great harm. We spend time learning lessons of when enough is enough. Practice forgiveness but realize it does not always mean we subject ourselves to dangerous situations. We learn loving boundaries, and we learn to break down walls that keep love from finding us. However to love one another is so important. We are so much more comfortable giving complaints, or voicing what is wrong with a situation or a person, which has its merits at times, however, why not start adding more sincere compliments, and pointing out more focus on the positives? It is great to do with a random person daily, or at work, and of course with those you love. No one will ever mind when you do! Opening and reopening the heart is a great lesson of love, it is a muscle that grows stronger when we use it. The ability to love again after being hurt, or the ability to love while hurting is a most masterful and beautiful heart.

If you are a giver and empath, setting healthy boundaries helps to protect yourself. Building healthy boundaries helped me against those that chose to practice victimization, blaming others, lack empathy or responsibility for their actions, sociopathic, or narcissistic behavior. Walk away and let God handle them. How do we connect with Spirit? How can we feel or see something? Sometimes it is so hard because we can't see God or feel Him, but can we? I can only share how I do. God is appreciated in everything and everyone that is loving and beautiful. He is in the open and in the details. I enjoy the adventure in life and finding and connecting to God's light, and noticing it is all around us everyday and everywhere. It is all around us like in a sunset, trees, and all the work of art in nature. It shines within us, like in a baby's smile, a warm embrace or holding hands, or an act of kindness. It works through us when we chose to open our hearts and allow it.

Romantic love causes amazing feelings of connection with each other. We all do not escape the devastating heartache of romantic love at least once. A true love will add to your life in a positive way and appreciate all the things about you. If you find yourself hurting to often for periods of time from your romantic love, and have needed to walk away, but have not been able to, check your level of self love and care. Sometimes people wear you down. Walk away. Heal. Please honor your self worth.

NATURE

Nature is a place I go for healing. Nature is a great place to meditate and pray. I am often led to go there often for connecting and healing. It teaches us about the natural rhythms and cycles in life. I would go to nature as often as possible to get in touch with myself and Spirit. It is a great place eliminate all the outside influences and "the noise" or stressors. Drinking enough water helps to hydrate my body, it brings me a full mind, body, spirit adventure. Walking in nature brings great connection. I love to find a spot that feels inspirational and sit comfortable to notice the heavenly sights and sounds all around using all the helpful senses given us to connect. I am able to feel God's love in all the beautiful details surrounding me. I then breathe in and let if fill my body. Upon exhaling, I release and imagine all the negative is released. Inhaling through my nose, and exhale through my mouth. If there are times its difficult to inhale through the nose, then your mouth is just fine.

I find trees to be so amazing and I love to learn about them. Once I saw the big tree in Heaven, ever since I felt a connection to learning from trees and I enjoy their folklore meanings. When I touch a tree I can fee its healing energy.

BE A CHILD

Be a child! Find the simple fun in life! Children have endless bounding bursting energy and so much more. I believe you don't need to be rich to have fun! Sometimes the best fun is in every day tasks. You can have fun cooking and maybe have a playful fun food fight once in a while, or sing while cooking! I choose to add fun along the way and somewhere in the day. Remember how to play? If not, it's okay. Just think of the things that you used to like as a child. Take a walk down memory lane and think of the things you enjoyed as a child. Examples can be playing an instrument, singing, dancing, painting, riding your bicycle, playing catch, swimming, coloring, fishing, knitting or crocheting, rock collecting, riding a motorcycle, walking in the rain, stepping in puddles, talking to a friend, shopping, hiking, spending time by the river, writing, or photography. Take the time to realize that you are loved and cherished and to love yourself enough to have some fun!

Children say the funniest things because they remind us of what is important that often times we forget. Children say it refreshingly and offer insights. Talk to a child and ask their advice! I always said children are as wise as adults, as adults we just have more experience. Experience is often learning lessons from getting burned in life. It can close us off in many areas as adults where a child remains more open. They have a more pure and open heart. and a less cluttered mind and vision. I enjoy being silly, talking in funny accents, and doing imitations of movie scenes. Being child like reopens my spirit to having fun along the way.

GIFTS

Gifts are endless. I find the beauty of gifts come with humility, and are practiced humbly. Here are a few we can notice in ourselves and in one another. They include listening, hugs, knowing how to get the perfect gift, making someone laugh, paying a compliment, the perfect comment, a warm smile, doing a simple helpful task for another, healing, gardening, picking up pollution along the road, showing appreciation by saying thank you, forgiveness, teaching someone something you know, building things, fixing things, counseling, healing, being on time, being reliable, being responsible, honesty, compassion, kindness, being organized, trustworthy, stability, being silly, making someone laugh. Add your special and much needed light in the world. You are valued. Knowing your gifts is simple; it begins by listening to the feedback you get in the world when people appreciate something about you! It is also a journey to find and recognize your own gifts. Loving yourself and taking care of your health is a most important gift to yourself and others. It's important to take care of our vehicle.

It is gift when we tell others the gifts we appreciate in them. Have fun and sit in nature with someone you enjoy, and bring food you have cooked together while singing, and dancing, then plan to share all the things you appreciate or notice in each other. Take off your shoes and stick your feet into water, a river, sand, or grass. It has to be something grounded and natural. Connect your feet to the earth, your hearts to each other and use your minds to help communicate with the best words you can find! Watch your spirits lift higher! Practice how it all ties together for a full mind, body and spirit experience.

ANIMALS

Animals are so much simpler than humans. They have eyes that let us see exactly what is in their hearts. They are not like humans at all. They have much more predictable patterns and predictable behaviors when studied. Some people have told me they are more comfortable with animals then humans and they trust them more.

I can understand why. Animals are used in certain hospitals as therapy. They lower people's blood pressure and light up their spirit. Sometime they even give people a reason to live. There are Seeing Eye dogs that assist people in great ways. Animals showed me how they trust and love and how much we can learn from them. I love the way my dog greets me special every single day and lives in the moment. People have asked me if I saw any animals in Heaven and I have to say I personally did not, but that doesn't mean they are not there.

Animals bring me inspirations and reminders throughout the day that improve my life. The dolphin is one of my favorites when at the beach or boating. The breath and manna of a dolphin reminds me of the cycles of life and the high levels of communication. The blue heron represents introspection. When I see a blue heron I am reminded to reflect on something and practice introspection as the blue heron shows me he is usually alone and does not gather in a group. The bear reminds me of power and hibernation. I am reminded go into hibernation or a meditation of my own and take a moment to find strength. The beaver builds a damn. It gives me a reminder within my own life and to look at what I may need to build or build upon. The deer crossing my path reminds me to practice being gentler during the day. I love the way certain cultures honor animal spirits, and honor the love and wisdom they bring. I believe the way the animals have a food chain also teaches us lessons about the importance and purpose of life cycles.

HEALING TOUCH

Without human contact, infants fail to thrive at birth. We can give them nourishment; clothing, safety, and medical care, but without being held and rocked and without having human contact, and an infant will eventually die. This is a medical fact. This is how we are made.

People are searching for attention, to be held somehow, to accept and embrace differences, listen to concerns, judge less, and have fewer friends concerned with appearances and meaningless things. They long for less texting, fewer emails, and more talking, sharing stories, more dinners at the kitchen table, remembering the power of healing with touch.

We long to be close to someone, to know if others can see us, to know if we can see them, to know our inner beauty, and to learn to trust someone. Many of us feel very broken and damaged; have doubts; and feel lost, unloved, or rejected. After listening I recognized there is always a need to be connected with someone. There is hope someone can see us through all our guardedness. Some people will pay for someone to give them attention, to listen to them or notice them. They can even pay to be cared for when they have no family or friends, or feel hopeless, misunderstood, lost, confused, and beaten down. Maybe they feel rejected by a church or have lost faith in God because of a few people who judged their clothes or appearances. So maybe they feel abandoned by the church, and think God or Heaven is too far away.

It's right next to you. He is right next to you, and you can talk to Him all day, every day if you want to. Many in service classes are given in hospitals to teach the power of touch, as well as the power of healing hands, holding hands, and hugs to relax and comfort, heal and soothe.

ENERGY

I saw energy as a child in the way the living things carried light. I witnessed and experienced how divine light carried information and love. When I studied sciences during college, I had the memories of my experience relate to the science. Here I saw science and spirit merge. The light had energy, love is energy, water, plants, and all living things have energy. Time is energy. Energy is within everything. Our words, body language, and expressions have energy and impact one another, both positive and negative. When words have the power to cause someone to be wounded, I call them word injuries. Body language carries information and energy. It validated the responses I had, for example, when I meet someone and was on guard for no apparent reason, or when drawn to someone who has a beautiful loving energy.

Energy impacts. We can become aware of our energy, and make a choice of what type of impact we would like to give and receive.

Also we have to do our own work to clear out our own negative energy so we can be open to receive. I think many people who are givers can often give love and help, but have trouble receiving it because of past issues causing mistrust or feelings of unworthiness. I can tell you that you are so loved it is beyond anything I could have ever imagined. Imagine if you could live your life letting all the negatives go, and trusting in the love that is there for you. I felt the most intense divine love from Jesus's hands and have experienced that complete purity. I call upon it often to enter me from head to toe, and please know you can ask for it as well.

LIVE IN THE MOMENT

How do we live in the moment? I hear things like I'm so busy. I had a bad day. I'll wait until a few years from now. I'll do it when I'm retired. The weather isn't right. I should do this first.

Living in the moment doesn't mean to panic that this is your last day on earth. It is a beautiful way to increase your happiness and fulfillment in life. It is a way to wake up in the morning and become aware of your day. It is simply not going through the motions. I remember when my children were small how I would appreciate their hugs in the morning, but not the chaos of getting ready for school. Now they are older and I appreciate the coffee I can drink in silence. It's your mind that can help you to live in the moment.

Living in the moment begins with waking up and tuning in to what you have going for you. It may be only an hour, or ten minutes within the day, but don't miss it. Living in the moment matters because life can change on a dime. I remember making promises that I will never complain again, if you help me get rid of this pain. The beauty of physical pain is we forget about it almost immediately after it is over. . So if you wake up with a body that feels good and has no pain that is a good moment. The car has no gas, the alarm didn't go off, your bills are overwhelming, and all the irritations that can happen, but learning to stop ourselves and remember that the sun came up and you are here, and you have another gift of a day. How many people would give anything for that? Moments can be missed. Living in the moment means priorities. Try not to miss your child's basketball game, or birthday party. Try not to stay home and clean and miss a beautiful day at the beach. If you have a chance to tell someone you love him or her, don't miss the moment. Say I love you often. Make that call. Love someone more because it might be the last moment. Its simply just not taking time for granted, and I sadly see it as a kind of insult to those who have less time. I wish there was a way to give it to those who appreciate it.

I wondered why we wish we were at a different time in our lives? Statements like, I wish I was younger, I wish I was a kid again, I wish I was older, I wish I was in my twenties or thirties. Why does it seem to me we often are never really happy in the moment, and want to be in a different place? During those ages, I think we were wishing to be in other places. You are in the perfect place you are meant to be in this moment. If you are unhappy just make the decision to make a change. Sometimes we are being prepared for the next moment. Everything can change on us in a moment, and we can make changes in a moment. It really is that fast when you put your mind to it. Embrace the here and now. Looking all around distracts from what is right in front of us. Seize the day and cherish the gifts that are special for you. Imagine how wonderful it would feel to let go of all the expectations in our heads and just breathe deeply for a moment.

CHAPTER 34

HEDY'S PASSING

My Mom….

I kept my promise; I never left her. I went to place my hand on her cheek when she couldn't speak from her brain tumor (she had aphasia), and I crawled into her bed with her in Bon Secure Hospital, the one in New York where I was after my skiing accident. Funny how we both wound up there since we both lived so far away from that hospital. I don't believe it was a coincidence. I put my hand on her cheek and sang our childhood songs. A tear rolled down her face, and her eyes said so much, even though she couldn't communicate. I looked at her with all the love we can hold in our eyes, and the music we can make. I kept my promise and never left her.

She passed a few weeks before I went to my thirty-year high school reunion. I received comfort from seeing my old friends again and remembering my childhood. It was a little like being home again with Hedy: her hugs; her smiles; her warrior-like protection of me; and her advice, which I appreciate now more and more, as I didn't have to work so hard to develop boundaries when she was alive because I had her. I since have been developing my own.

Unexpectedly this giant box inside my chest opened and continues to further open this day. My secrets were no longer bound by a promise. I now got the guidance, or calling to open up spiritually and write it down in a book. I thought the idea of a book was interesting, as I didn't ever like to even write birthday cards. I trust that it was the way chosen for me to honor the message I received so I wrote this book.

CHAPTER 35

THE HEART ATTACK

It took many years to finish writing this as it was difficult to relive it over and over again, and then putting it into words was very challenging. Life also was very busy so time got away from me. During the last few months of writing, I started feeling pain in the middle of my back. I thought it was just muscle tension since I wrote a lot while sitting on the couch, in poor posture positions. I used pain reliever creams and didn't complain much since I know nurses can get bad backs from years of lifting patients.

Anyway, shortly after I finished writing this manuscript, I went to an oral surgeon for a tooth extraction. Greg was driving calmly, and I was looking at the most clear blue sky and the mountain ridge. I looked at my husband and said, "I'm going to say a prayer out loud on the way to the dentist, okay?" We both kind of were surprised and smiled. It was a routine visit and friends advised me to get my back pain checked and to get my teeth done as I was putting it off for too long.

Greg said "Okay."

I asked Jesus, God, and all the angels, to help me have a safe doctor visit and allow it to serve my highest good. I asked them to keep my health safe and let the doctor do the right thing and bring me where I need to go.

After I arrived, the dentist checked my blood pressure. He said it was way to high to do the oral surgery. We waited a few minutes to see if my blood pressure would decrease after a few deep breaths, but it got higher. So he sent me to a cardiologist in the next building. The cardiologist saw me right away. After tests, he said I needed an immediate cardiac catheterization. My cardiologist had my confidence the entire time; he was intelligent, thorough, and kind. His intelligence was matched by his amazing ability to keep a frightened person calm. He knew how to win my trust. I also trusted that I'd prayed in great faith.

The doctor who was supposed to perform the catheterization said he was unable to help because of the difficult location of the widow maker blockage, and suggested I go to Johns Hopkins immediately for open-heart surgery. I had a widow maker heart attack, which most people don't survive, along with blockages in the widow maker artery. So an ambulance rushed me to Johns Hopkins. When I arrived I was in the best of care with the most knowledgeable, caring staff.

Late that night I began to feel tightness in my chest. When I rang the nurse, she began administering medications and then she called the surgeon and his team to come in earlier than I was scheduled. Turns out, I had a 99 percent blockage in two places. I remained calm, with controlled breathing and total focus on my faith. My family's presence there was such a blessing.

Early Easter Sunday morning, the open-heart surgical team came in. I prayed out loud for them and asked God, Jesus, and all the angels to give them clarity to do their job well. I prayed for my family to have faith and strength, and for myself that I would come if He was calling me home, but I really wanted to stay longer with my family. I really wanted to live and I trusted God would do what was best, and I prayed using my voice, and asked out loud if I could stay. After the surgery, my surgeon said we definitely had "some help" in the operating room, and looked up as he said it. The conversations in the hospital were open about faith. Greg smiled, shook his head, and said, "I'm not surprised. I've never seen this in a hospital, all the hugging, the warmth, and the speaking of praises to above!

The most amazing, smart people I must say took care of me at Johns Hopkins Hospital. They were amazing. The nurses were brilliant, and all those who study so hard to help others deserve to hear that they are deeply appreciated. All those years of study are appreciated as well.

I survived beautifully, and after taking time to heal, I debated whether I should get the book published. So I prayed with my neighbor. One day I told Eric I was afraid to do the book, because maybe the heart surgery was sign I shouldn't publish it and share it. I was scared after such a big surgery to do anything that would jeopardize my health. He said, "Mom, one has nothing to do with the other. Do it. Publish it." Eric always has a few words that stick with you because they are so genuine and knowing. He has a gift of that and when he shares it I am grateful. I will always be proud of his brilliant mind and generous heart.

I came home with the added benefit of having my son; Gregory sacrificed to help me recover. His patience and support was life enriching. He made me feel so safe and encouraged me everyday. He never made me feel handicapped, he made me feel so normal. He buffered the trauma of the experience and never doubted that the normalcy in my life would return. I never worried about being alone or afraid as he assisted me with anything I needed while providing me with trusting, uplifting and healing companionship.

> Christine's strength and maturity, her hand on my face, her saying encouraging things to me, at her age were amazing signs of such a good girl. She expressed appreciation that

> I lived, went to school every day, got good grades, and got me drinks and whatever else I asked her to get for me. She didn't argue and that's amazing for a teenager. And she held me. She knew how to calm me when I was overwhelmed.

Eric came to visit when he wasn't working. His biggest challenge was driving the long distance to see me, but he was right there when I was going into surgery, and his hugs are amazing and protective. He usually says very few words and with big meaning.

All my children made me feel like I had the best team of healers. They were all supportive and giving. I am so thankful, And Greg, my husband, was so helpful and never once left my side, not for a day or a moment. He was there every day and slept every night in the hospital with me until we went home. They are my people, and my team, and I have an incredible group of close family and special friends. Cherish them and love them as often as you can. They gave me the road to recovery, and I could do my work, and share this story with you now.

Love and miracles are always a universal language we can all celebrate together and connect to light up or recharge. We should record and celebrate our present day miracles; and just in case you have forgotten to believe in miracles, always remember you are one. May you always find your way to shine your beautiful light. Enjoy life and have some childlike fun along the way, and remember to love each other.

The end. The beginning. Agape.

CPSIA information can be obtained
at www.ICGtesting.com
Printed in the USA
BVOW03s2253201217
503356BV00001B/178/P

9 780998 811918